Dear Joh

Thank you,

...man kind. People like you

...hange the world, one word at

...time,

STAND OUT FROM THE CROWD

HOW TO GET MORE LEADS AND CLOSE MORE SALES JUST BY BEING YOURSELF.

How to stay relevant in a world of technology and stand out from the growing crowd of sales agents.

CARMEN BADAN

With Love and Gratitude,

TABLE OF CONTENTS

Part 4:
The Distance Between Comfort Zone And
Success Is Called Massive Action

DEDICATION

I thought dedicating this book to my mother and father would be cliché, so I actually was not going to write a dedication. Then one day, I had to submit a live video for a challenge on a Facebook group I am a part of. The mission was to share with the tribe why I believe I am a miracle. Seriously? I thought. That's a little arrogant. Yes, I believe in myself and the whole nine yards, but a miracle?

And then a light bulb went on in my head. Of course, I am a miracle. I am alive.

I am grateful to my wonderful parents not only for loving me and caring for me and for doing everything possible to see me succeed but for supporting me through good and bad and being my energy and my source of power and my guiding light and my DNA. Most importantly, I am grateful to them for giving me that one-in-400 trillion chance to be here today, healthy and happy and to be writing a book.

Yes, I dedicate this book and any other book I'll ever write to the amazing human beings called mama and tata. They are the reason I am the happiest woman alive today.

They are the reason why I wake up every morning with a smile on my face and say to myself, "Is this for real? Am I actually living this life or am I in heaven?"

I am grateful to them for choosing not to do something completely different in that fraction of a second when I was conceived.

I could have been someone completely different. But, by the grace of my parent's love and affection for each other, I am not. I am Me. And nobody can take this away from me. And nobody will, not even me.

Mom and Dad, thank you for giving me, Me. I promise to never disappoint.

I love you.

And I thank you all for reading this book. Please know that I put my heart and soul in it, and I am here to support you and be your cheerleader.

To your success,
Carmen Badan

INTRODUCTION

70 billion dollars are paid to real estate professionals every year in commissions. Tech real estate companies would like to get their sticky little fingers on this money and push the middle man out of the picture. We, the real estate agents, are the middlemen.

I wrote this book for all the hard-working real estate agents out there who are afraid of what the future is going to bring.

I know you're scared that the robots are threatening to take over your job.

I know you are tired of hearing news of Zillow and Trulia and Realtor.com selling your own leads back to you. You don't want to pay them and yet, you need a source of leads.

You are probably afraid of companies like Redfin, Rex and OpenDoor. You have a good reason to be afraid. They are after your commissions and your very livelihood. These companies have massive amounts of money pouring in from venture capitalists prepared to "disrupt" our industry. They will not stop until they clean us up and destroy our careers.

I was in the same boat. There was a time when I did not want to pay my Inman subscription because I was afraid to read all the bad news. While Inman, as a source of industry news for real estate agents can be valuable, it seemed to have turned into an avalanche of news highlighting changes designed to eliminate real estate agents. Then, one day when I saw an article online showing buyers letting themselves inside a home, welcomed by a lovely lady speaking from an iPad perched on a stick. Her voice was gracefully giving full details about the home and at the end, she asks them to make an offer. And by the way, before they went inside the home, these buyers were already pre-approved for the loan. It's not a nightmare although it may become one day for any of us who don't believe humans can't be replaced.

That day, I decided to do something about it. I decided that nobody is going to make me lose my job unless I decide to leave the industry as a matter of my own choice.

To make matters worse, in the past five years the number of real estate agents in the country has increased by about 30%. However, only 10% of the agents are still doing 90% of the work. There has also been a downgrade of our wonderful profession to simply an occupation rather than a career. What a hard pill to swallow.

So, how do we stay relevant, I wondered. I had to figure out a way to stay in the business and stand up to the tech companies. I decided not to go down without a fight.

Regardless of the many changes, we all face as technology moves further into our lives, I know one thing for sure: nobody can take away my drive and my love for the business and my customers and clients. I had to find a way to show that I care and that nothing can replace the value I bring to the table.

I started paying attention to what was happening around me. What are my customer's needs and wants and how can I meet them? Where are my clients hanging out? Wherever they are, I need to be there and show them that I care. Not tell them but show them. Anton Chekhov said, *"Don't tell me the moon is shining, show me the glint of light on broken glass"*.

And one day, it hit me. There was only one way to reach my clients: show them that I care through video on social media. Eureka.

It was not easy. I had to overcome a plethora of limiting beliefs, but I did it and my business is better than ever.

I wrote this book for you all because I care about you and your amazing profession and because I want to encourage you to believe that nobody can take your job away from you if you want to keep it.

If I can do it, so can you.

With gratitude,
Carmen Badan
The Stiletto Broker

FOREWORD

Hey, Realtor... what's your future? This question, alone, insinuates that your future may be out of your hands. It suggests that some cosmic force may determine *your* fate in *your* industry, like it has in others. Are you willing to go down without a fight? Some days, I imagine taxi cab drivers standing on the streets of New York with their heads cocked like dogs listening to whistles, wondering what the heck happened when Uber entered their world. Will we be the same?

Carvana is a cool way to purchase a car without a live salesperson. Shop and purchase on your computer, the car is delivered, and you may try it for a week and send it back if you don't like it. Exit the salesman with the bad rap, the "used car salesman." Self-checkout at Walmart is not a new concept. Kiosk check-in at the airport is old hat. Flat-screen ordering at Panera, faster than ordering in person. When was the last time you stood in line at the bank to see a bank teller? Technology strikes again! Taxi cab transportation was ripe for disruption, enter Uber. Real Estate is ripe for disruption. Already entered and well-established on the scene are Zillow, Google and Amazon, among others. It's a scary bird's eye view of man vs. robot. Enough to make a bird bury her head in her nest and never come out again!

Yes, but that was before the bird read this inspiring perspective on the balance between standing out from the crowd and staying relevant. Like walking a tight-rope between "should" and "must," real estate agents have to stay wanted (maybe not needed, but wanted), and must clearly rise to the surface in a sea of competitors. This task seems huge, illusive and daunting with more than two million wandering around out there. So, maybe some will give up? The pages going forward scream "DON'T!" Instead, read on! You'll be utterly encouraged and moved to adopt a secret ingredient in your relationship with customers that ultimately defies logic.

Consider this example ... my friend's wife travels quite a bit for business. She chooses to use Uber, of course, for condo to airport transport when she travels back and forth from Minnesota to Naples. Here's the key, she has *one driver*, that she calls all the time in Naples and one in Minneapolis. Why? Because she trusts and likes that driver. Ah ha! The faceless robot gets defeated, and the relationship between customer and service-provider is still alive and well, even in the ultimate, automated world of transportation.

Likewise, my dad and I drive different car brands. When he goes to get service, he arrives and types his name into a kiosk, leaves the keys in the car and goes inside to the waiting room. Good enough. When I arrive, one of three guys who all know my name, opens my car door and greets me warmly. They transport my briefcase to the waiting lounge for me where my table is "reserved" because my service rep knows I like to work while my car is serviced, so he puts me at a quiet table with USB ports and phone charger ready. He also has a Diet Coke waiting for me, every time, and asks about my son, Dalton, by name. The attention my service rep gives to my needs is what has me driving past 50+car repair shops between my home and the dealership to have this experience. They call it "creating loyalty beyond logic."

You can create that for yourself, too, and *Stand Out from the Crowd* nails how. Recognizing that we aren't all born rock-stars, Carmen Badan's account of her own development is relatable, energizing and refreshing. Her constant, "If I can do it, so can you," theme is like a strong hand reaching out to pull you through the waves of digital marketing to a place where you design and define yourself—opening the best gifts of yourself up for your customers to discover, desire and demand. Once you create demand, you will defy logic, and a demand for you separates you from the crowd.

Kerri Elizabeth Herrity
Founder, ARES, Inc.
Business Development Coaching

PART 1

HOW I WENT FROM TWENTY DOLLARS IN MY POCKET TO A SUCCESSFUL REAL ESTATE BUSINESS AND HOW YOU CAN DO THE SAME.

CHAPTER 1

THE WORLD IS CHANGING

The world is changing. If you have been in the real estate business for over fifteen years you can say that you've seen it all. You have experienced the boom, the bubble, and the bursting of the bubble back in 2008. You have seen foreclosures and short sales and bankruptcies and investors swooping in to pick up foreclosures at garage sale prices. You have seen a comeback and a slowdown.

You have seen technology taking over every single aspect of our lives. You have email addresses and desktops and laptops and smartphones.

Your smartphone is not just a way of communication, it is a media tool. It has replaced everything from maps to dictionaries, to newspapers, to TV, to radio stations, to photo and video editors, and so much more. Your cell phone has become a part of your body and your life.

At any given second, your phone is within an arm's reach. Most of us sleep with our phone by our bed. For some of us, our phone has become an addiction, but that's a different book. At the same time, we cannot ignore the fact that this tech revolution brought about by our smartphones is also our biggest opportunity to stay relevant in this business and be in touch with our clients at a moment's notice.

While these days I approach technology with ease, when I was a student in Romania I did not like computers. We had limited access to technology. In fact, computers were just introduced in my last year in college and we were allocated one computer to six-to-seven students. It was so basic and antiquated, and it made absolutely no sense to me. I was not interested in "playing" with it. Everyone wanted to have me in their group because they got to play more. I thought: who needs such a clunky machinery to play games and write letters. Little that I knew that one day I will be writing a book about embracing technology, making it an essential part of our career, and using it to stand out from the crowd and survive in a threatened business environment.

Yes, I learned to embrace technology because I realized early in the business that there is no going back to the pre-smart-phone-era. The question is not if we are going to be taken over by technology, the question is how soon will it happen? So, as Americans say, *"If you can't beat 'em, join 'em."*

As a real estate broker, I started using video early in my career. My original videos were bland, involving only photos of the property. I was progressive in 2007 but they did not cut it in the new era. I learned that I needed to put some skin in the game if I wanted to make a difference and stay relevant. I needed to expose myself and there were no two ways about it. Even though my business was doing great, I felt that I was not connected enough with my clients. After I learned that by 2019 over 80% of web traffic would be claimed by video, I knew I had to step up my game.

I was truly scared. Video. I was definitely not inclined to start getting in front of the camera. There was a time in my life when I was afraid to make a phone call for the fear that the other person will not understand my Romanian accent or what I was saying. Or, worst I wouldn't understand them, and I would sound like an idiot when trying to respond to their questions. Yes, fear has stopped me from my growth in the past but this time I was determined to win.

I took the bull by the horn, overcame my *limiting belief* about having a Romanian accent and did it. I started to create my own little videos on new listings, open houses, community info but also stepped outside the box creating cooking videos and inspirational content. I learned more about myself in one year from creating all these videos than I ever knew before. One of the things I learned is that my friends on social media, many of them my clients, enjoy hearing from me. They watch my videos, they comment, they like and share and most importantly, they reach out to tell me that I make a difference in their lives.

My personal and professional growth became more than a job and a natural progression, my growth became my mission. By putting myself out there in front of the public, I am able to influence and support the growth of everyone I touch. And from here, there is no going back.

The best part about opening up and getting involved in social media with video marketing is that I learned to believe in myself and even more important, I learned the importance of giving and caring. My business has been booming ever since and I find that I actually work less hours than ever before. I have time to travel, time for myself, time to expand my horizons, and time to learn how to diversify my business, as well as time to write this book and start online seminars.

I can tell you one thing for sure, ever since I opened up and allowed myself to grow, I have not asked for business unless I was approached by someone. And yet, business is following me around like a private eye following a cheating husband. My business is better than ever, and I feel that everything happens effortlessly.

How did I go from a rugged, unedited first video to

thousands of followers and people who look forward to my next post? I decided to start moving towards my fear and not away from it.

CHAPTER 2

HOW I GOT HERE

It might look like I've got the world by its leg now but trust me, it did not use to be this way. I've come a long way and I have scars to prove it.

I was born in Romania and grew up under a communist regime. At the age of seven years old I decided that one day I will move to America. I lived in a country torn by inequality, lack of freedom of speech and expression, lack of basic needs and necessities and the capacity to contribute to the society and under a permanent shadow of fear and uncertainty. The only thing I was certain of was my parent's love and hope. Lots of hope.

I remember myself as a child playing in front of our apartment building. I was ten or twelve years old and I would hear a rumor that there was meat or cheese, or other basic food being delivered at the local grocery store. I would quickly grab the key hanging around my neck, underneath my shirt just to check that it was still there, just to make sure when I ran up the stairs and I am in front of my door, I don't discover that I've lost it.

I would put my hand on that key knowing exactly what the next steps would be. Run upstairs to the second floor, open the door, go in my parents' bedroom, look under the sheet of paper placed neatly on the shelf in their clothes closet. I would grab the money I found there, grab a bag, and run to the store while letting everyone I ran by know about the food about to be delivered so they can also have a chance to get a place in line and feed their loved ones. But not before I would call my mother at work and tell her what the plan was so that she knows that on her way home from work she should stop and get in line with me so we can have a chance of getting double portions.

I would run downhill towards the grocery store, about five, six blocks away. I would see the big line of people waiting from a distance with anxiety and disappointment. But I wouldn't give up. I would run there and get in line behind the last person.

As soon as I would get in line, I would announce loudly, "I just want to let you all know that my mother is coming from work and she will be joining me in line." This was done as a precautionary action in order to avoid being yelled at in case my mother would get in line and I wouldn't have announced her arrival. I cannot describe that glorious moment when we would both be able to buy two rations of food. It felt like a major celebration. It felt like I had been able to help my family survive, it felt like I have been able to provide for my people. It gave me the sense of responsibility, gave me the sense of duty, and it gave me the sense that every action matter.

This childhood experience has built in me a sense of caring for others and a sense of teamwork. The sense that *if I win, you win*. The sense that if we both win, then the whole world wins. It has built in me a sense of leadership, a sense of taking charge, a sense of taking care of everyone around me, the sense of tribe.

I was a good student. I was a little bit of a geek, if you ask me. I was the shortest in class, I was skinny and flat, I had long ponytails, very long almost down to my hips. I wore eyeglasses and I carried a backpack, a red, hard, pig-leather backpack all the way through my school years until the end of high school at the age of eighteen. Yes, I was a geek.

My dream was to become a nuclear physicist and as luck would have it, in spite of my outstanding grades, excellent knowledge, and determination, I failed the exam. I thought that the world was coming to an end because of it. You would bring the subject up and I would start crying.

I felt like all my dreams are crushed. This was my

first failure and I did not know how to handle it. I did not know what to do next. So, I went back to the one thing I knew how to do and that was study.

I spent an entire year at home with my mother studying and crying. I don't know why but my mother, trying to motivate me, I guess, would sometimes tell me, "You know, if you don't want to study and become someone, you don't have to. You can always get a job at the public restrooms by the stadium." I know she meant it as a joke but this hurt me more than being punished in any other way.

I was truly disappointed in the Nuclear Physics university because it turned out the principal teacher in charge of the subjects for the exam that year had sold the answers to a group of affluent students. This came in as a shock a few months later. He did go to jail for it which vindicated me in a way, but it also woke me up to the real world. Wow. This is possible.

Since I was gifted with an equal amount of right brain and left brain, I was also very creative and really good with making clothes. And my next option, a summer later, ended up being textile university which I graduated five years later with an engineering degree, a fashion design and marketing specialty.

The anticommunist revolution that shook the entire eastern world happened in 1989. I was in my second year in college and I thought that everything is now going to be all right. We are free, we are capitalists and we are now surrounded by opportunities . . .

Not so fast. My country had to go through a painful process of cleansing itself first, while under a new, corrupt government. What a disappointment for many of us looking forward to a better, different future.

At the start of the revolution, I thought I was meant to get involved in politics. I was already holding a position in the leadership of my university class and really was always holding court everywhere I was, as I still do. I was getting involved in events, watching every speech, having an opinion about every meeting and demonstration, only to realize that it was all rigged. It was a coup, an organized crime if you will. The bad guys got rid of the other bad guy. This felt sort of like they fooled us. What are you going to do now, suckers?

As soon as I finished university and had the guts to start my own business. Well, I had no choice because the factories where we were meant to all get jobs were ran by the government. Since the government, the way we knew it was obsolete, all factories were all closing down or being bought by foreign entities.

I had absolutely no clue what I needed to do in order to run a business, in order to start my business. Instinctively I knew that I needed to focus on what I loved to do, I needed to focus on my skills.

What was I good at? I was good at making clothing.

I was good at creating, designing and actually sewing the garment. I started to make clothes in my parent's apartment. One of the skirts I was working on required a special tool to create pleating. I found a small co-op in town, who had the machine and went on to meet with the owner. He was running a clothing firm that looked exactly like my dream except he was the owner.

He liked the fact that I had an engineering degree and he said that he needed someone like me in his firm. I said I was not looking for a job and that I am opening my own firm and working on my first collection. He said, "Why don't I come and work for me until you are ready to open your own business?"

My intuition and my mother's intuition helped us conclude that it will be a good idea. By working for him I got to learn the ins and outs of the business, while I was providing him with a lot of value as well.

A few months later, when I finished my collection and sold out of it in two days, I knew I am onto something. Turns out, Romanian women were hungry for something different than the standard communist era stark couture. They were hungry for color and style and haute couture and I was there to offer it to them. At that point, I gave up the job, I hired a couple of young girls to help me on the sewing machines and started my own company.

I was working fourteen hours a day and I had

fabric dust all the way up my nose and inside my brain. Fabric dust was running through my veins, it felt like. I would blow my nose in color depending on the design I was working on.

I have no idea how, I stumbled upon a Libyan fabric distributor, who was located in Bucharest. I went to see his warehouse and mesmerized by the beautiful colors and patterns of the unique imported fabrics. I remember passing my hands over every single roll of fine materials, inhaling the scent of brand-new fiber, feeling the delicacy of the silks and viscose, under his keen observation and hungry eye. But that's another story.

The dream had started to form, and I proceeded to visualize a new collection. This time I thought "A real fashion show" Why not? As crazy as it sounds, I could see myself walking on stage at the end of my very first fashion show to the music of Tina Turner. *"You're simply the best"* Was this delusion of grandeur or was I just a big dreamer?

My accountant, who was also a good friend of mine, was a university professor and she suggested I sponsor the Miss University Ball that year. This seemed like a great idea so, I met with the young beauty queens and took their measurements. At the Ball, these young beauties were wearing my collection, and it turned out to be the most beautiful pageant a school in Romania has ever seen. The success was great, but it occurred in a very limited environment of professors, deans and students. I knew I wanted more.

My next thought was that I needed to do a fashion show on a runway ... why not? Just like in the movies, with models and music and photographers. There would be media coverage with an article in the paper and a spot on local television ...

I needed models. To find them, I went disco dancing one night, but I did not really dance. What I did instead was approach a few young girls on the dance floor and asked them if they would like to be fashion models? They asked me why I came to them. I told them because they had perfect bodies for a fashion show.

What I did not tell them was that they had perfect bodies for the dresses I already created. I needed them to fit in my dresses, I did not have the time or the money to create new outfits for the runway. They all said yes, and this is how I produced the first independent fashion show in the modern era of my town. The event was amazing, and it ended with me walking down the runway in a bright pair of orange stilettoes, an orange linen short and bra combo with a black sheer man's style blouse with satin cuffs and collar with Tina Turner's music cheering me on. I looked and felt like I was ready for the big world. I don't know where I came from that I could think something like this up and actually make it happen, but there I was, bold and gutsy and unapologetically savoring my success. And this is how I launched my fashion career.

From that point on, I started creating collections that I would sell in local boutiques. I also had a clientele of some of the most well-off women in town like lawyers and doctors and judges and professors. All of them eager to show up every day at work or at a special occasion wearing a Badan. I never advertised and you could not get to me unless you were introduced by someone already in the circle . . .

I was also a regular guest on a Sunday talk show, as well as teaming up with a friend who was a reporter. She came to me one day desperate and said, "Carmen, I need your help, if I don't come up with a good idea for a show, I'll lose my job." I said, "Let's do a show where you interview me about good ways in which women can revamp their old wardrobe and make it look classic contemporary." We were a big success. She did not lose her job and I was offered a job on TV. I did not take that job as a felt it was not my calling.

An investor reached out to me one day out of nowhere and asked if I'd like to start a partnership with him. He said you are the brains and I am the money. We can do something amazing together. I had no idea how this was going to work. The concept of investor was completely new to me. I had no business acumen, the only thing I knew was to follow my gut. I said no.

With all of this success, I still felt like something is missing. I was not where I was supposed to be. I couldn't quite find my place and I did not know why. I just knew something else was out there for me.

It just so happened that my fiancée at the time ran off with one of my models, a young girl I had taken under my wing. She was stunning but not the smartest cookie in the cookie jar. That didn't seem to matter to him at the time. I knew her story though and I knew she was really in love with another guy, who, incidentally, was not ready to commit to her.

One day, I called her. I said, "All I want from you is to know why you did it? When you and I both know that you love this other man." Her answer was that she wanted to have what I had. Thus, the highest form of admiration came disguised as betrayal. A lesson in love, trust and generosity . . . check.

He did come back one day asking for forgiveness. I just did not have it in me anymore to be with him. Nothing was fitting in anymore. I just could not figure out what it was until one day when it hit me like a bowling ball.

My friends and I were hanging out one evening playing pool, drinking beer and smoking cigarettes. I wasn't a smoker but the way my friends were, I might as well have been . . . I was about to hit my last ball and I vividly remember hovering over the pool table, one with the cue, squinting my left eye, cigarette smoke penetrating my nostrils and my mouth, imbibing my skin and my clothes in tobacco.

One of my friends said, "Hey, do you guys know Laurent Blar? He left for America" I hit the ball so hard, my last ball and the white ball went in the hole . . . I looked up and said, "How did he do it?"

A little side note here. Remember that Romania had been under a strict communist regime and even after the revolution, we were still considered pretty much a third world country. So, the concept of taking off and going on a trip to America or any other western civilized country was totally foreign. America, this is how we called it, not the United States . . . to us it was America, the land of opportunity and of dreams come true.

My friend chucks his cue, takes a deep pull out of his cigarette, gently places the cig on the edge of the table, leans over the pool table getting ready to break and while he reluctantly lets the smoke out of his mouth knowing that it's going to go straight into his eye, he says, "He took a job on a cruise ship"

Two months later, I was interviewing for the job of bar waitress with an English-speaking answering machine.

I had never worked as a bar waitress before. I had never even worked in the service industry, but I needed to give the Americans, who were coming to interview us, proof that I knew what I'm doing. Let's just say that I produced references from a few restaurants I worked at in my home town.

Well, the references said I worked there. There was only one restaurant on the list of LLC's. A pizzeria we always ate at and the owner of it was willing to sign a reference letter for me. The others were friends of mine with a stamp, not real restaurants. I wrote the letters, translated them and they put their stamp and signed them. I did the same for my two of my friends who took the leap at the same time with me. It had to be done.

CHAPTER 3

WELCOME TO AMERICA

So, on October 31st, 1995 I fell in love with Florida's heat as soon as I stepped outside of the Miami airport. First stop, Miami Beach at the Fairmont Hotel on Collins Avenue. This was an old hotel owned by the Chandris family. They were also the company running the restaurant business on Celebrity Cruises. They were my new employer. I was a crew member. This was scary and exciting all at the same time. The plan was for all the new crew members to do a couple of weeks of training in the hotel before joining a ship. Basic accommodation and cafeteria food were provided, which was a good thing because all I had to my name was twenty American dollars and a $500 debt to my parents. The trip cost me $2,300, which was the equivalent of two years' worth of salary in Romania.

As I arrived at the hotel, I dropped my half-full duffle bag in the room equipped with 2 sets of bunk beds, changed my clothes and went downstairs. On my way to the hotel, I had been so mesmerized by the buzz on the streets, the restaurants with outdoor seating and the bright store lights that I decided to take a stroll and check things out. After all, I finally was seeing my childhood prophecy come true. It was time for me to touch it, smell it, taste it, feel it.

On my way out of the hotel lobby, the nice man at the reception stopped me and kindly asked where was I going. I said, "I just want to go for a quick stroll".

He said, "Be careful out there." And he shook his head in disbelief. I did not pay attention and walked out the sliding doors. Cool. Sliding doors. As soon as the steaming heat of the street hit me, it dawned on me . . . air conditioning. Wow . . . civilization.

So, I stepped outside thinking to myself, "I made it."

I was about to do one of those Laurel and Hardy heel clicks when Collins Avenue made me do a double take. A convertible limousine was just driving by and it was full of young cheerful people dressed in costumes. Masks and feather boas and large colorful glasses and bottles of champagne in their hands. Must be some special celebration I thought, some carnival going on. Good for them.

I turned to the right enjoying the beautiful October evening breeze not even knowing I was only one block from the ocean. As I reached the corner and was about to cross the side street, a large van without front doors was making a right turn exactly on the street I was about to cross. A dark-colored van full of people dressed like vampires was suddenly in front of me. I saw them clearly because they slowed down barely four to five feet in front of me. And while the van was turning right, a tall man with a long, black gown and a white mask on and with fangs stretched his right arm out towards me holding on to the rail in the doorway with his left hand. He looked into my eyes and said, "Come with us, sweetheart." His face seemed to flood with blood, and I stopped in my tracks. All of a sudden, I felt like Alice in Wonderland. What's a nice kid like you doing in a place like this?

Well, well, I might be coming from a third world country but sure as hell, I did not expect this type of welcome.

I made a quick 180 and stepped right back into the cool, fresh, welcoming hotel lobby. The nice gentlemen at the reception lifted his head up and said, "That was quick." I answered him and said, "Actually, it turns out, I was more tired than I thought." And then I headed straight to my room.

This was my Halloween *Welcome to America*. It was a year later before I was going to find out the meaning of such a strange holiday, because at the time

I never dared to talk about it for the fear of being considered stupid.

My roommates, at the hotel, were two friendly and bubbly girls, one British, one Irish who were always talking 100 miles per hour in a language I had never heard before. It sounded vaguely like English but not the one I learned in school. I would catch one or two words every now and then when they were addressing me, I would nod and smile, too embarrassed to admit that I had no idea what they were saying.

There was a lovely bar in the courtyard of the hotel and the crew was hanging out at the bar every evening, drinking, smoking and laughing. I was not drinking unless someone insisted and offered me a draft beer. Nobody knew that I was holding onto my last twenty dollars like I was holding onto my life. It was right there in my pocket and I would touch it from time to time to be sure it was still there. Twenty dollars never felt so good.

As the days were passing, my pals were saying goodbye, and were happy to take off and join their ships and start making money. I was still there two weeks later. I was becoming a fixture as far as I was concerned, and I was starting to worry that I'd never receive an assignment to a ship so I can start making money, until one day.

My name was finally on the board next to the

cafeteria, I was checking daily. I was assigned to go to the Zenith one week later. It was a smaller, older Celebrity Cruises ship, but a five-stars ship. Woohoo. Time to celebrate with a beer at the bar. Four dollars later, I came to my senses when the thoughts of a big list of items I needed before embarking hit me like a brick wall.

I needed stockings, deodorant, shampoo, conditioner, soap, feminine products, a comb and hair gel. Next day, still excited, I strutted into a small pharmacy on Washington Avenue, a short walk from the hotel and filled my basket up with everything I needed. On my way toward the cashier, I remembered my twenty-dollar bill. Well, twenty minus the beer.

I looked at my basket full of beautiful American products and started to do a quick math: two pairs of stockings about eight dollars, deodorant, four dollars, comb, a dollar seventy-five, hair gel, five-fifty, feminine products, six-fifty, conditioner and shampoo, eight dollars. Total, thirty-three dollars and seventy-five cents. Turns out I was a little short. Seventeen dollars and seventy-five cents short.

A cold sweat hit me, as well as the painful realization that the shiny contents of my basket would have to be gently placed back on the shelves . . . I wanted to cry . . . I felt crushed; I felt defeated; I felt shame. I wanted to crumble to the ground and cradle and cry.

I placed every single item back on the shelf, one by one. The shampoo that took me so long to decide on it, the matching conditioner that smelled so good, the pink box of feminine products, the hair gel that looked so glamorous, the blue comb, the Secret deodorant that smelled like baby powder and finally the stockings. Do you know how long it took me to figure out the size I needed? We did not have these sizes back home in Romania. I had to calculate, measure myself with my bare hands, guess, ask around. It was a process.

I spent time, energy and dreams on those stockings. I saw myself wearing them looking classy in them. They were the right color for my skin and the right texture. I opened the box, I touched them and felt them, I smelled them. Stockings have a certain smell, a smell of elegance and sophistication, a smell of accomplishment and I loved that smell.

I always loved that smell even back home when many times I had to resort to stopping a running stocking with a drop of nail polish, even when I knew I had a small hole forming at the top of my big toe and I would walk gently all day to keep it from further damage. The bags of tights I kept and never threw away because maybe, one day I will take them all and have them repaired . . . I was putting the last pair back on the shelf and tears were rolling down my face, and then it hit me, I am keeping the stockings. I am keeping one pair of stockings. I needed them. I needed to feel good, I needed to feel accomplished. I opened the box and smelled them again and smiled, like saying hi to an old friend I did not see in a while. I closed the box and put it in back in my basket. I was happy.

Blood was starting to flow back through my veins. I wiped my tears making sure nobody sees me. I started to do the math quickly in my head energized. Stockings were a must: four dollars. Deodorant . . . I couldn't live without it, four dollars. Feminine products . . . are you kidding me, six dollars fifty.

One dollar and fifty cents left according to my algebra. I needed shampoo, badly. I once washed my hair with soap and I promised I'd never do it again if I can help it, but there is no shampoo for a dollar fifty cents.

I took a deep breath, closed my eyes, exhaled and headed back for the hair product shelves . . . 7.99, 6.25, 4.99, 3.99, 2.75. My finger was reading the labels because my eyes were in tears. There was no fear left, there was just strength and stubborn determination. I knew it had to be there. This was not the end of it. And all of a sudden . . . eureka . . . one dollar thirty-seven, red label . . . on sale. A small bottle of VO5, "Clearly not the best shampoo if it was on sale." I said to myself, but who cared? I was jumping for joy. Later, of course, I learned more about American marketing strategies and adapted to looking with anticipation for the red labels.

I pranced over to the cashier and handed the little old Jewish owner my sixteen dollars. The total came in at sixteen dollars and seventy-five cents . . . what? It must be a mistake. I almost fainted when he pointed at the cash register. "Taxes", he said. Oh, no. I did not think of that. All of a sudden, I remembered the beer from the night before and the bartender had given me change. What did I do with it? I was wearing the same pair of shorts as I was the night before, so I stuck my fingers in all the pockets and found it. I pulled out in disbelief three quarters. I needed four more cents. I looked in his deep, friendly eyes and somehow, he knew. He reached out to the little jar on the counter and grabbed four pennies and threw them in his till. He handed me the receipt. I thanked him and ran out of the store before he was going to change his mind.

I made it. I was yelling out loud in my head. I made it! I made it! I stopped and crumbled in a roll on the side of the building, crying.

I made it!

America . . . here I come . . .

So, why am I sharing my story? Because it is a story of resilience and resourcefulness and never giving up in spite of the unfair life conditions, and child programming.

It is a story of constantly stepping outside my comfort zone in order to make steps forward towards becoming successful. By doing that I was able to break through a myriad of limitations and rules I was conditioned with based on upbringing and the cultural differences I experienced.

And if you are a real estate agent in today's world, I know how you feel. Technology is taking over so whether you are new to the business or you've been in it for a while and you feel that you haven't sung your last song, you feel overwhelmed and scared and worried and you don't know if you will make it. And I am here to tell you that if I made it, so will you.

And this is why I am writing this book, to share with you how some regular immigrant with a heavy accent, afraid to drive or make a phone call was able to cut through the thick and thin, embrace change and technology, and build a serious real estate brokerage and start a legacy.

PART 2

READY TO LEAVE YOUR LIMITING BELIEFS BEHIND AND START MAKING A DIFFERENCE IN YOUR LIFE?

CHAPTER 4

THE GIANT TECH ELEPHANT IN THE ROOM

Let's get this straight. There is one thing we did not take in consideration as far as two to three years ago, and this is the giant tech-driven real estate companies mushrooming to take what is yours. Your commission.

Whether we like it or not, it is time to address the elephant in the room. Real estate tech companies are deploying billions of dollars to develop technologies aimed to push us out of our own industry, our own business. Yes, we got a taste of it when giants Zillow and Trulia swooped in with one sole purpose, which was to put real estate agents out of business in 2006. You might not know this but Richard Barton, the founder of Zillow is also the founder of Expedia. Expedia was the nightmare of every travel agent in the country because all the services that travel agents provided were now available to consumers at a discounted rate at the push of a few keys. Expedia, although we, consumers love it and use it because we enjoy getting a deal on travel, put travel agents out of their business. Barton and his partners employed the same tactics when they started Zillow in 2006 and the only reason they did not succeed is because the timing was wrong. The market had crashed, and they had to take a step back. But rest assured, they may look like they are playing nice now, don't be fooled. The concept is not dead, and they are at it again.

Zillow's days as a nightmare for real estate agents are not over. You can read this article if you would like to.

http://articles.latimes.com/2006/feb/08/business/ fi-zillow8

Just recently we heard in disbelief that not only is Zillow is buying homes now, but they also have purchased a mortgage lender to start helping with their plans to flip homes.

A simple Google search will take you to results that will make your hair stand up on the back of your neck. From the automated showings that eliminate buyer's agents to sophisticated robots sitting in million-dollar homes acting as the listing agent to massive investor-driven online property management companies offering rentals and managing portfolios for investors. It is all here. It is all happening as we speak. As much as we want to ignore it or pretend that robots will never put us out of business, remember the billions poured into these companies as they seek to become the market maker and control this industry. They have a relentless drive to succeed. But most importantly, what works in their favor is the desire for buyers and sellers to save money. For instance, on a million-dollar listing, if they use a tech company, a seller can save a minimum of $30,000. This is real money.

In addition to the massively-funded tech companies, we are also faced with an exponential increase in the numbers of licensed real estate agents. Every one of your clients who looks at the financial statement and sees that you just scored $9,000 in commission as a result of helping them buy a $300,000 home, will say to themselves, "Wow, she made $9000 for showing me seven homes? That's a lot of money. I am in the wrong business. I can do that." And next thing you know, they call you for advice on where to hang their real estate license. There are over 1.3 million real estate agents, members of the National Association of Realtors in the United States and this number is growing every day. According to Tom Ferry, a celebrity real estate coach, 87% of all real estate agents fail. So, this is the time for you to stand up and not be a statistic. It's your time to shine and make a difference.

But, if you think that your job is safe, think again. Now, I am not telling you all this to scare you. This is not a scare tactic. This is true, factual information, you can Google in seconds.

The good news is, you as a real estate agent, have the tools necessary to keep yourself in business. You just have to shift your thinking from being a real estate agent to becoming an expert service provider who cares, listens, and understands your client's needs and has a well-crafted solution for them.

And this is what this book is going to do for you. Teach you how to stay relevant in a world of technology, stand out from the growing crowd of real estate agents and gain loyal clients who are willing to pay for your expert work in spite of the temptation of saving money.

What you have to do is to be willing to come out and play, even if the playground is outside your comfort zone.

CHAPTER 5

MINDSET

The first step in becoming a relevant, successful real estate agent is shifting your mindset. Yes, it's that simple.

Start believing that as long as you do your best in every circumstance, as long as you are constantly bringing value to your clients, there will be no way you will not become successful.

In his 1910 book, *The Science of Getting Rich*, Wallace Wattles said, "Your true worth is determined by how much more you give in value than you take in payment." You might as well have this tattooed on your arm because as far as I am concerned, this will be the motto for years to come. It is the fundamental principal that will bring every real estate agent success.

Stop selling real estate, yourself and your twenty-two steps program and start adding value to your client's lives.

Psychologically speaking, people act based on pain or pleasure. The way they act or react, what they accept as a status quo in their lives, is influenced by their relationship with pain or pleasure.

Once you master the use of these two feelings you will be able to understand and bring value to your clients and their lives.

Once you are able to extract from your clients what is it that moves them, what is it that makes them tick, what are their needs and move towards satisfying these needs, you will master the business of selling. And that is selling not only real estate, but you will master every negotiation you are involved in including the best price for your new vehicle.

Another important shift in your mindset is turning your job into your mission. Vishen Lakhiani, in his book *The Code of The Extraordinary Mind* said, "The most exciting people in the world do not have a career. What they have is a mission."

They say that people don't buy what you sell, they buy why you sell it. A great Ted Talk to watch is *Start with Why by* Simon Sinek. In his talk, Sinek provides incredible and brilliant insights we can all use in our business.

You can be the best salesperson in the world, but until you have a *mission* that is in line with your client's values and until your sole goal is satisfying their needs and wants, your sales skills and your hard work will only keep you feeling frustrated and defeated.

Finding your way is one of the most important steps for any human beings. As *Mark Twain* said, "The two most important days in your life are the day you are born and the day you find out why."

So, take a sit and dig in. Take a pen and paper and start writing. Figure out WHY you do the things you do? What is your purpose in life? Why do you wake up in the morning and keep going?

If you need help figuring it out, go back and read Napoleon Hill's *Think and Grow Rich*, listen to Vishen Lakhiani's three most important questions on YouTube or just any other old way to keep asking yourself WHY until you get to the bottom of it.

Once you know why, you start to reverse engineer your message to your clients. In order to get what you want in life, you will find that you must first help your clients get what they want in life.

So, instead of the standard cliché, instead of selling yourself as the best real estate agent in your area, the one who is able to produce the best results in the shortest amount of time by employing proven marketing techniques to sell your client's home, your new approach may be something like this. I believe that my clients deserve the best service and personal attention and my only job as a real estate agent is to make you happy, to be on your way to your next adventure in life, or to put your feet up and sip on a cocktail on the back porch of your new home. My job is to listen and care about your needs and wants and follow proven strategies to sell your home or to help you buy a home.

Your mission to bring your clients happiness while buying a home and your belief that they deserve the best professional service are your WHY. Your why is the reason people will want to work with you.

Finding your why is the first step in discovering your authenticity.

CHAPTER 6
LANGUAGE AND BEHAVIOR

Next in line, you have to evaluate your relationship with money and success.

Yes, it might sound strange to even bring money up, but I am here to tell you that the majority of the people in the world have a poor relationship with money and this reflects in the way they conduct business, themselves and the way they dream. Your relationship with money is not something you just developed. This is the result of your beliefs inherited from your parents, your teachers, your religious leaders, your life partner, your family, your business partner.

If you are one of those people who think that money is the root of all evil, that the rich will be richer, or that if they are rich, they must be thieves, or that the richer they get the poorer others get, it is time to shift this thinking right now. Because until you change your mind about money, you will not attract it. You can go ahead and read this paragraph again.

So, start shifting your mindset when it comes to your relationship with money, with high-end properties and high-end clients. Start owning it.

Start accepting the abundance that is heading your way. Start accepting that you deserve to be successful. That the wealth coming your way is not making another person poor. That you are just getting what is already yours.

Start with the end in mind. Decide what your end goal is and trust that you will achieve it. Make that goal big. As they say, if your goals don't scare you, they are not big enough. Make your goal your mission in life. Find your Why and the How will appear.

Neville Goddard, a new thought author, thinker and philosopher said, "Think from the end, not of the end." Wake up every day telling yourself that you've already succeeded. Walk and talk as if you are already successful.

Conor McGregor has been named The Most confident man in the world. Have you ever watched him walk? Watch him do it until it gets in your blood. There is nothing more uplifting than watching Conor McGregor strut like he owns the world.

Mohamad Ali said, *"I am the greatest, I said that before I knew I was."*

These are the people to follow, these are your confidence role models.

Think it, believe it, and you will achieve it. It's that simple. Don't just allow the thought to come into your mind. Invite it, welcome it, embrace it, be proud of it, talk about it and own it, believe it.

Your subconscious mind doesn't know any better, so it will signal this message into the Universe and you will attract exactly what you keep telling yourself.

I know what some of you are saying now, "I am a realistic guy, I can't lie to myself." This is not lying to yourself. This is believing in yourself. This is do or die.

Believe in yourself even when no one else does. Believe that millions are coming your way. Someone said, "If you don't see millions in your imagination, you will not see them in your bank account."

When David told himself that he would go out and beat Goliath, did he lie to himself? He went out to face Goliath and he won. He used unconventional strategies, a stone in a sling, and he won. He did not lie to himself, he believed in himself. The result proves it.

When Alexander the Great brought his men on the shores of Persia in 334BC, they were overwhelmed by the size of the Persian army. He asked his man to burn their boats, "*We will either go home in Persian boats or we will die fighting*" was his call to his soldiers. Failure was not an option.

They burned their boats and beat the Persians. Time for you to burn your boats.

Now, most of you, the experienced agents out there will find that you are already following all of my suggestions. So, this part is not necessarily for you. But all of you, new agents joining the ranks of the business, finding it a struggle to integrate, learn the business, make sales and stay relevant in spite of the huge competition, this chapter is key.

It is time to believe in yourself. Believe that you can do it. Believe that the deal is done, the commission is already in your bank account. Tell yourself that every day, morning, day and night, and act as if it has already happened.

Change your vocabulary. Shift your statements to express gratitude instead of unhappiness. When a client cancels a meeting, instead of getting upset be grateful that you get more time to work on your business and prospect for a new client who is really serious about buying or selling.

Never let NO take you down. Always, always give yourself a chance. A lowball offer comes in? Put in in writing and present it. You never know where it will end up, just put out the good vibes and it will happen.

When your client says this is my final offer, unless they specifically ask you to tell the other party, don't fight it, just present it and let it unfold. You will be surprised to see that your client has another bullet in their chamber. Don't lend your ears to naysayers.

My husband, whom I love dearly in spite of the fact that he is a realist (and I am going to leave it at that), is also a licensed broker. He was working with a client who was in the market for a million-dollar home. After a whole year of showing him properties and answering lengthy emails and battling Zestimate, my husband was ready to drop the client. "Not worth it", he said. The client was a retired mergers and acquisitions broker. He was a tough cookie. I took the challenge and two years later I helped him, and his wife move into a beautiful $900,000 home. Was it easy? No. There were sleepless nights during the negotiations, there were rejections, tears and lots of frustration, but I got the job done. And the hard work and stress did not bother me as much as everyone's doubts that he'd ever buy ... But he did. I turned helping him buy a house into a mission and I never gave up.

I am that one agent who showed a couple eighty-four properties in seven days. They did not know what they wanted so every day we were changing criteria. I never gave up. I loved them. I love all my clients. I am grateful for all of them. Without them, I would not be here today.

So, every day, armed with a new list of properties to show, I kept going and probing and checking in with them to see if we are on the right track. We were looking at condos and townhouses because they were adamant that this is what they wanted. Then, the last day, with my bag on my shoulder and ready to go out the door, I had a hunch. I sat back down at my computer and looked for a home that was at the high mark of their price range. I set up a showing on a whim. I printed the sheet and took off. Yes, my commission was going to be higher, but I did not do it because of that. I did it because everything they wanted fit in the description of a home, not a condo. At the end of the day, they were tired, and not really excited about any property in particular but they decided, reluctantly to make two offers. A condo and a twin villa, both short sales, not always a good outcome. Then, on our way to the hotel, I convinced them to take a look at this one more property even though they were tired. So was I. But we went to look at it. I will never forget the wife's smile as she walked in, touching the walls of the foyer, opening her arms wide into the open and bright living room, turning around almost in a dance. "This is it!" she said. The last home we looked at became their home. Was I happy? I was thrilled. This is what I live for in my career. To see my clients happy. To them, I am Wonder Woman.

And this is who you are as a real estate agent. Your client's hero.

CHAPTER 7

MASTER YOUR SALES SKILLS

Let's get something straight. You are not a real estate agent. You are a business owner and a marker. But most importantly, you are the creator of your Universe.

How do I know this? You are an independent contractor and you own your own future. Your future depends on you and not on anyone else. And, in order for you to be successful in your business, you need to have clients. Lots of them. How do you get clients? By being a good marketer. Your job is to get good at selling and get good at marketing.

One of my favorite sales books is *Sell or be Sold* by Grant Cardone. His notion is that it doesn't matter if you are a sales professional or not, at any given moment in your life, you either sell or you are being sold, every single time. In any circumstance.

And I am not talking only about being sold a product. Any situation in everyone's life, any conversation, any interaction whether with another adult or child, at any given moment you are either sold something or you are selling them something.

Whether you are trying to convince your loved one to marry you or your kid to eat his broccoli or your husband to take out the garbage or your adolescent son is trying to convince you to stay out past curfew, it's called selling. We sell ideas, we sell products, we sell services, we sell experiences, we sell beliefs, we sell trust. We sell tangible and intangible products.

Even right now, I am selling you the idea that at any given moment you either sell or you are being sold.

What really makes a difference is how we do it?

Real estate agents are one of those groups of people who, for whatever reason, they don't like to call them-selves salespeople. Yes, as if they would be somehow embarrassed to call themselves a salesman or a sales-woman. As if being a salesperson, somehow makes them sleazy and self-serving and disingenuous and appear as pushy and aggressive.

As if being a sales person is a demotion on the humanity scale.

What many real estate agents do, unfortunately, is start a conversation with a potential client by saying, "Don't worry, I am not a sales person, you can trust me."

So, let me ask you a question? If you are not a sales

professional, what are you? You prospect, you qualify, you take people in your vehicle and show them properties, you negotiate terms and prices, you do listing presentations, negotiate your commission, market their homes and the list goes on. What does it sound like? A tour guide, a concierge, a butler, a therapist. Well, you might be a therapist from time to time so scratch that ... do you see my point? No matter how you turn it you are a salesperson because you know what they say. If it walks like a duck and quacks like a duck ... you get the point ...

Anyway, if you insist that you are not a salesperson, I have news for you. They are not buying it, and if they do, it is actually to your disadvantage because if they are looking to sell their home or buy a home, they are actually hoping for a skilled salesperson, who can negotiate on their behalf and get them the best deal and terms when they buy or the most money when they sell ...

Did I make my point?

Good.

So, let's all agree that we are all salespeople here and that's okay. Not only that there is nothing to be ashamed of, there is nothing wrong with that, we are now free to act and benefit from the skills and qualities a salesperson should have. And once we have developed these skills, it is our obligation to be there for our clients.

Here is the catch. You are never to use your sales techniques to get clients. You are to use these tools to help your clients reach their goals.

When it comes to getting new clients, your job is to give them daily valuable content for free. Your clients are savvy. They have access to all the information online. They know what's available, they know what sold and for how much, they read every description of every property they are about to see . . . They don't need you for that. They need you to be able to explain and interpret data and information for them. They need your expertise in negotiating, in learning about all the steps in the transaction ahead of the game, they need re-assurance at all times that they are in good hands. That you are not asleep at the wheel.

And nowadays, in a world of technology, there has never been a better time for us, real estate agents to prove ourselves in front of our clients, we just have to understand that the dynamics have changed, technology is moving at a very fast pace and there is no going back. So, we need to get on board with it before we get pushed out by agents who embrace technology or by the robots.

So, now it's up to you to become not only the best version of yourself as a sales professional but also to make your mark in the industry by standing out from the crowd.

How do you do it? How do you get to have it all? How do you get to be successful? I have news for you. You stop thinking about you, you stop thinking about your money, you stop thinking about your success, you stop thinking about what this career will bring to you and what every encounter with your customers will put in your pocket, you stop looking at the commission field on the multiple listing services. You stop calculating your commission every time you take a client out in your car or every time you are submitting an offer, you stop worrying when a client decides to terminate an agreement you stop worrying every time you meet a customer and you just start thinking about what they want, you start thinking about their needs, their pain and their pleasure. You are not the only real estate agent out there. You are not the only one doing what you are doing. So, why should they work with you? They should work with you because you can ease their pain, you can help them reach their dreams, you can help them get what they want. And once you start thinking about your customer first, everything will start happening for you.

In *Secrets of Closing a Sale,* Zig Ziglar said something extremely powerful that has been a game changer in my real estate career: *"You Can Have Everything in Life You Want If You Will Just Help Enough Other People Get What They Want."*

The other way to look at it is this. When you want something, and you fear you might not get it, you act differently, your client will sense this bad juju coming out of you. You will act desperately, and your client will react to it. They will not even know why they react negatively to you, it will be their gut feeling. Humans have an alarm signal that is intuitive, and their alarm signal will turn on and they will react by walking away from you. They will smell your fear.

They say that what you fear the most, you end up manifesting. How many people get bit by a dog just because they approached it with fear? Dogs smell fear and they bite. Customers smell fear and they walk away, they dump you.

CHAPTER 8

MARKETING SKILLS

So, you are going to tell me now . . . wait a minute, I know nothing about marketing. I don't know how to market? Relax. That's why I am writing this book.

Here is the good news. Write this down. 90% of your marketing is being yourself. The rest, you learn from others. I am going to teach you a few tricks right in this book. In fact, I promise that by the time you finish this book you will have a whole new perspective of yourself as a real estate professional. You might even start walking like Conor McGregor.

We entered the technology era about twelve years ago, maybe a bit longer. Twelve years is all I have knowledge of thoughts because I started in the industry at the time of the real estate market crash and the internet taking over the real estate status quo. At least taking over the way traditional agents knew it and used it.

At that time, before I actually got my real estate license, my husband and I owned a real estate auction company and together with a group of auctioneer friends, we were doing luxury real estate auctions in Nevada, California, Texas and Florida. We were specifically advertising absolute auctions. Without getting into too much detail about absolute auctions because this is not the scope of the book, an absolute auction is basically letting the world know that the home offered at auction will sell to the highest bidder, regardless of the price.

The big difference between auctions, and traditional real estate transactions is this: at the absolute auction, there is one known factor, the date the home will sell.

The reason why I give you this information is because I want you to feel the difference between putting a home on the MLS, a sign in the yard, St. Joseph buried, a postcard sent to the neighborhood, an open house every two to three weeks and then and hope for a buyer in five to six months and an accelerated marketing strategy that procures a qualified buyer within forty-five days at most.

An accelerated marketing strategy means you have a significant budget and you throw everything at it without discrimination. So, as we were doing auctions back in 2005–2007, part of my job was to work on the internet marketing. This is when I discovered Trulia and Zillow and LoopNet and Realtor.com as well as a lot of auction related websites. Many of them were free and I was able to post every property and market it to the audiences on these sites as well as use the information in our weekly update to the seller. We were able to track viewers, number of clicks, etc. Our clients loved numbers, so they loved to see the progress of our marketing.

These aggressive marketing strategies helped me understand where traditional real estate marketing was starting to head after the crash of the real estate market. Full speed towards the internet.

Our clients are looking for more than just a list of properties to look at. As we know, over 94% of buyers start their search online. Sellers start online as well. They look for an agent who fits their criteria. And what do they want? They want an agent who is experienced and tech-savvy. Statistically, 85% of buyers and sellers choose to work with an agent who uses video as a marketing strategy. They don't like to be sold. They want local knowledge and insights. They want an agent they like as a person not just as a professional. They want to know who you are. They want to like you and then if they trust you, they will want to work with you.

So, how will they know who you really are? I know many of you have all these fancy designations and I salute you for that. But no, your name followed by your GRI, CSI, ADD, CCD, ACDC designations will not help ... They'll just roll their eyes and say yeah, yeah ... confidence booster ... but what's in it for me?

Instead, here's how you do it. You don't just tell them that you are qualified for the job, you show them. Let me repeat this one. You don't tell them, you show them.

How do you show them? You tell them your story. They will pick you because of your story. How do you tell your story? You look deep down within yourself and find out what makes you happy. What are you good at? What makes you smile? Is it your dog? Your cat? Your family? Gardening? Cooking? Shopping? Restaurant Hopping? Whatever makes you happy, bring it out into the light. Make it part of your business. Make it part of your story. Business and pleasure do mix. I'm going to call this *Bleasure* ...

And here is your Marketing strategy technique #1: Market with Bleasure.

The second marketing strategy is Value. Marketing strategy technique #2: Give value. Value, value, value. Don't ask for a sale until you give them value nine times. That's your formula: nine to one. Give them value 9 times and ask for the sale once. Remember to ask and not take. Pretty simple and you can't go wrong with it.

It takes a lot of work, but it works.

It is hard but so is staying broke, so which hard do you choose?

CHAPTER 9

CARE

I cannot tell you how much I've struggled so far in this book to not bring Gary Vaynerchuk's name up. Not because I don't want to give him credit for the many things, I learned from him in the past couple of years, but I am afraid that once I start talking about him, I'll never stop.

In case you don't know who Gary Vee (for the ones who can't read or write his last name) is, here is the short version of his story. His parents immigrated from Belarus when he was three years old. His family was crammed into a one-bedroom apartment until his father was able to buy a liquor store in New Jersey. He started to work in his father's store at a very young age. Gary discovered the internet and through his video blog and paid Google ads he grew his father's business from three million annual revenue to sixty million per year by his mid-thirties. He is now the CEO of a media empire, VaynerMedia. Some of their notable work includes video marketing for Budweiser, General Electric, Pepsico, Noosa and many more. Their main influencer media avenue is video. They call themselves a full-service digital agency built for the Now.

In his book, *Crush It*, Gary Vee talks about several marketing techniques he recommends to entrepreneurs in order to crush it with social media and in general to make an impact, leverage themselves for the most attention they can get and be the go-to entity in their field.

In his book, Chapter 9 is about Care. And he says nothing else about it. Just Care. And as I am writing this book, I realize that my chapter about care is also Chapter 9. Coincidence, or am I being guided?

How simple is that? Just care. Every single step towards marketing yourself and your business must be based on care for your audience, your leads, your clients. It's not about you, how good you are at what you do, how much experience you have, how many deals you closed, how big and global your company is or any other self-serving baloney. Nobody, I repeat, nobody cares about your amazing strategies. All they care is what's in it for them. All they care is about how much you care about them and what you can do to help them ease their pain or increase their pleasure.

As Teddy Roosevelt and John Maxwell said in their

discourses, *"People don't care how much you know until they know how much you care."*

And in today's environment, when we cannot hide behind a stack of papers in a listing presentation or a well-crafted website, or a beautiful business card, this statement is more relevant than ever. Because people will look you up online and they will find you and what they see will influence their decision on hiring you. Or not.

Care is the core of our mission today. Care is the cornerstone of all relationships. And you are in the business of building relationships.

And to quote another giant figure who speaks to my soul, Maya Angelou said, *"People may not remember exactly what you did, or what you said, but they will always remember how you made them feel."*

So, make them feel important, make them feel that you have their interest at heart, make them feel that they are the most important person for you in that moment when they interact with you, when they find you online, when they watch your videos, when they see your social media posts, listen to your podcast, read your book, when they get your emails, when they get a call from you. Make them feel that you care.

Once they know you care, they will shower you with love, loyalty and referrals. You'll thank me later.

PART 3

IT'S NOT TOO LATE TO FIGHT BACK

CHAPTER 10

WHO'S AFRAID OF THE BIG, BAD WOLF?

Artificial intelligence has been infiltrating the real estate world for years. First through virtual design by creating full virtual 3D tours of homes as well as virtual staging. A virtual 3D tour is truly helpful to buyers of new construction as it helps them visualize how their new home is going to look before the builder actually breaks ground. The technology is so sophisticated and realistic that in many cases it is hard to figure out that the home is actually only in the imagination stages, artificial reality.

Virtual staging, on the other hand, comes in handy to real agents marketing a vacant existing property. If the sellers have moved out and home is empty, in order to make it more attractive to buyers, virtual staging comes in handy as we can place virtual furnishings inside existing listings photos, and we make the rooms look attractive and welcoming. This technique has been proven to increase the number of showings on a property as well as increase sales prices. It has always been accepted and embraced by the real estate community.

And here comes the But. Yes, there is always a But. What comes next is going to make your hair stand up on the back of your neck. We are now watching artificial intelligence in disbelief as it invades our lives. And while being able to turn on your TV to the exact show you would like to watch when you want to watch it, or to adjust your home AC system without getting up from the couch or to turn on the hot tub from afar sounds appealing, when robots are stepping into our real estate world, threatening to take our jobs, it is getting a little too close for comfort.

I am concerned and I know you are concerned too. The speed at which technology is taking over our lives and disrupting industries, chances are we will be put out of our business by a bunch of Alexa's at a discounted rate in the next three to five years. And this, my friends, sucks.

And, if you are like me and you make a living from your real estate career or you just started this wonderful new life as a real estate agent, I am sure you are asking yourself every day, how do I stay relevant? How do I fight back? How do I stand up to the roboagents?

I know how you feel, I have been there. I have worried. Every day for the past three years. I read the

Danger Report released by the National Association of Realtors in 2015 and could not bring myself to believe that there is a 100% chance that real estate agents already shaky career and reputation will be threatened by a massive influx of new agents within four years(already happening) , 87.5% chance our commissions will decline within 3.5 years (already happening), 60% decline in our relevancy and 32% chance that tech companies will be taking over within three years. I have not seen a more recent Danger Report, but I am sure the tech companies are showing up to the closing table a lot more than predicted.

So how do you do it? How do you stay relevant? How do you keep your career? Here is the simple answer. By being yourself. By showing up for your clients and letting them see who you are and what you are going to do for them and how you are going to solve their problem. No roboagent can care about your clients and their needs the way you can.

Here's the thing. We go through life doubting ourselves and constantly wondering if we are doing the right thing or if we upset someone or if we are being judged and this permanent worry sucks all the fun out of life. Why can't we just be ourselves, funny, silly, goofy, loving and show up in the world as ourselves instead of trying to impress everyone else by emulating some persona we don't know, until we don't know who we really are anymore.

So, stop with the elevator pitch and go with your story. Your story is your ticket. Your story matters. Good, bad or otherwise, it matters. Make your audience feel something, make them matter and you will start to matter. Be vulnerable. Be You.

In order to stay or become relevant, you will have to start acting outside your comfort zone. You will have to decide between staying comfortable or being successful. The choice is yours and the good news is it is free. You just have to start now.

And I am here to give you all the tools you need to get started. Why I am doing it? Because when I started in this business, I was so clueless I did not even know that I could ask for help. I just wish I could have tapped into someone's experience and get some mentoring and learn the easy way. I did not even know there was an easy way.

When I started in this business, I paid the $29.99 and $69.99 for every coaching and sales techniques and lead generation technique I stumbled upon online ... you name it, I signed up for it. You name it, I signed up for it. I was so hungry to learn I spent twelve hours a day reading and learning and jumping from system to system. I just wish I would have figured all this out sooner. Well, let's just say, I had a hunch but fear of acting outside my comfort zone stopped me from taking action. I played it safe, I was comfortable, and I stopped growing. As Tony Robbins said, *"You're not growing, you're dying."*

CHAPTER 11

HOW I STARTED MY REAL ESTATE CAREER 1 BPO AT A TIME

As I mentioned before, I started my real estate career in 2007. Exactly as the stock market crashed and the real estate bubble burst. I had no idea it was actually happening because I did not have the experience of another crash and because it did not happen overnight. We had a feeling that something was going on. My husband had a hunch. And when I say hunch, I mean he was telling everyone, yes everyone that these prices cannot be going up anymore. Of course, he was the pariah because of it. People thought of him as being crazy, negative, pessimistic, etc. It was just his survival instinct talking and he was right. Yes, he was painfully right.

At that time as a new real estate agent with absolutely no experience in the industry, I had no idea what to look for when joining a brokerage. I was hoping for some advice from an experienced agent or broke, but I also was determined not to share my commission with anyone, so I decided on a brokerage advertising 100% commission.

I found them and went for an interview. I was anxious and worried that I was not going to get accepted because English was not my first language and I had no experience in the area. I was on full alert when I sat down with the broker, who actually made me wait in the conference room half an hour before he showed up. It's okay since I was so nervous, I almost did not want him to call me in. He finally came in the conference room, rather distant, asked me a few questions, sort of technical, I thought and then told me to go and see Jennifer at the front desk, give her $275 and she will sign me up.

That was strange and all I could think of was that I must have made a good impression. Extremely pleased that I was accepted and happy to call myself a real estate agent, I pranced out the door, got in my little red, pre-owned Mercedes and started making plans for my real estate empire.

My first few months were just the usual steps that real estate agents make, such as registering with the local area MLS, signing up for classes and seminars, reading real estate related books, dreaming about becoming a real estate mogul, practicing yoga and that's about it. As far as doing any real estate transactions, I had absolutely no clue where to start and where to end and the worst part was that every agent I met in seminars was complaining about the market and how they are not doing any business and how nobody is buying.

Needless to say, I started to doubt my decision of becoming a real estate agent. Nobody was selling anything, and the subject of all conversations was bankruptcy, foreclosure, short sales and bank owned properties. What could this mean, I wondered? How can I break through all this negativity?

And then it dawned on me. I thought the reason why I am not doing any transactions is because I did not have a website. Bing! All I needed was a website and then I'll start doing business . . .

So, I went online and after a little bit of googling I found this wonderful company. Some agents still use it. They had some beautiful templates you could use, fill in the blanks with some content, upload your pretty picture and voila, you had a website! I chose mine, NaplesBestHome.com. How appropriate. It was $19.99 per month, what a bargain.

I ordered new business cards because you know, your domain name had to be on the business card. I was pleased as punch and every single day I was googling my website. Naples Best Homes. But nothing was happening . . . hmm. . . . what's going on? I'd put it in the url www.naplesbesthomes.com and breathe a sigh of relief because it's still there. Phew, that always gave me a scare, but then I wondered, why doesn't it show up on the search bar?

I called the company and they said it takes time, it will not show up right away, just be patient. They did not have an exact idea of how long this would take so every day, I was on my computer searching for my site, Naples best homes . . . nothing.

A week, two weeks, a month, two months. I started to panic and feel discouraged.

I went back to my best friend, Google. I asked Google "Why isn't my website showing up on Google?" And here's what Google said, "because I was using a template". Me and 1500 other real estate agents, we are using the same template. A template is a bad word in the world of internet. A template means duplicate content. Google doesn't like duplicate content which means Google doesn't like templates. When Google discovers a new website on the internet, it gets excited but when it finds out that it is nothing but duplicate content, it trashes it automatically. What a rude awakening.

That did not sound good and now I did not know what to do next. And I wanted so badly to make it in the business. I just had no idea who can I ask for help. By then I had realized that my broker was not in the real estate business, he was in the real estate agent business and that was okay, as far as business model, it was just not ideal for me and my goals.

One day, friends of ours from West Palm Beach came to visit. They brought with them another couple. Melissa, our friend's friend, a lady in her early forties, started talking about internet marketing and how she is building a website by following an online tutorial with this guy, Steve Webber. She was not a computer whiz by any stretch, but she said he was very easy to understand, and he spoke in lay terms. She told me that if I wanted to have my website found on the internet, I had to build it myself, from scratch. She said I needed to use a computer program called Dreamweaver. My husband overheard the conversation and pitched in "Hey, I think I have an old copy of a Dreamweaver on my computer ... if you want, you can use it."

He also mentioned that a while back he had purchased a domain name called foreclosurenaples.com.

I was sold. The next day I was going to sign up for the program and start building my own website.

Please know that all this conversation was happening over plates of food and glasses of wine and beer and nobody was really taking me seriously.

The very next day I signed up for the course.

Four months later foreclosurenaples.com was up and running. From scratch. With search engine optimization going on. Within three months I was on the first page of Google. Ah, reunited!

Of course, I had no IDX. I did not even know what that was. The absolute only lead capture on my site was a small box for leads to enter their email address and a call to action, "sign up for a free list of foreclosures." I was not capturing names, phone numbers or any other lead information. Well, I wasn't asking for phone numbers because I thought, what's the point? I was not going to call them anyway. I was afraid to call. I was afraid I wouldn't understand what they were saying and worsts afraid that they would not understand me. I was embarrassed because I was ashamed of my accent and my lack of full understanding of the English language. Everything I was doing, I almost wanted to be incognito, like I was in hiding. I did not believe in myself. I did not believe I can do it. I thought, how can these people wanting to spend hundreds of thousands of dollars on a property can trust me with their most precious investments. If I only I knew then, what I know now. How could I possibly hold myself to such low standards? Sometimes it is painful to think about it but then I remember that I did finally break through that pattern of low self-esteem and I am grateful for the journey instead.

I was getting 3000 unique visitors every month. I had a very low conversion rate because I had no idea how to work the leads. What I did not know back then is that the money is in the list.

Once you have the list, you actually use it.

So, word to the wise, everyone you encounter goes on your list. You will want to take every call and even if you don't have something to sell them right away, put them on the list and keep them engaged. One day, if they don't do business with you, they will know somebody who will. Break your list into categories: hot, nurture, closed, pending, archive, etc. Think of these as niches and approach them differently in your marketing. As they say in the business of marketing, *there's riches in niches.*

One thing I was not afraid to do is to work hard. Since I was far from making money the traditional way, I spent every available hour on the internet trying to find any other ways to make money in real estate. So, I discovered the BPO's. You know what they are: broker price opinions. Well, a fancy name for a $50 bill. Okay, sometimes it's $70.

And, a little side note for the newbie real estate agents, since the market had crashed, there were a massive amount of foreclosures and short sales on the market. Banks would want to have an independent broker opinion about the value of each property they were either preparing to list for sale as an REO (real estate owned) or as they were negotiating it as a short sale. Banks were using asset management companies to do their marketing. What you had to do as a real estate agent was to sign up with hundreds of companies and hope to become their preferred vendor. No, signing up did not mean to open an account with email address and password. No, it took at least a half an hour to fill out forms, click buttons, upload files, etc. It was a labor of hope and unconditional optimism and a huge investment of time and energy.

Ideally, after doing a number of BPO's for an Asset Manager, you would start receiving orders to list bank owned properties. This was really the goal and the dangling carrot. My dream was to eventually get some listings out of the deal but for now, I would have been happy with a few BPO's, just to tide me over because our savings were going out the door and there was no money coming in. Really, I would have been happy if someone would at least answer my emails or my calls. Yes, I actually got desperate enough that I was making calls . . . holy smokes . . . Here's a clue, *desperate times lead to desperate measures*. I was burning my boats. Just a perfect example of human nature at work. While I was comfortable, I was afraid to make calls, when the times started to get desperate, I took the bull by the horn and dared to become vulnerable. And, you know what? Good news. I survived.

So, one day, after about two to three months of

continuous optimism and relentlessness in filling up forms, a sense of desperation hit me.

I had no stamina left. I did not want to give up hope, but I had to get out of the house ... I always knew that sometimes in life, you have to step back and look at the problems from the distance. You can't see the elephant if you are too close to it, you have to step back until you see the whole animal and then you can analyze it.

So, I grabbed a captain's chair and went outside. It was a beautiful sunny day. I grabbed my cell phone too. It was my first cell phone, a lovely, little red Samsung sliding phone. Every time I opened it, I would push the sliding part and it would make a really soothing noise ... sleek.

I sat in the chair next to a grafted citrus tree I had bought for my husband for his birthday and stretched out letting the warmth of the sun soothe my body and my soul. Tears were rolling down my face, my neck and running inside my ears. I opened my eyes and looked at the sky, tapped on God's shoulder and with a big sigh, I said, "God, something's got to give."

I decided to relax for a few minutes and think of nothing, just be there enjoying the sun. I was thinking about the beautiful art of grafting a tree to give oranges, tangerines, and lemons. What a brilliant idea. My husband had been in really bad back pain, so I bought him this tree to make him feel better, as he had always wanted one.

And speaking of my husband, what are we going to do about his back? He could not even stand up, let alone drive or do some work. I really needed a break. And a breakthrough. Not even five minutes into this whole avalanche of thoughts, my phone starts vibrating under my leg. I nearly fell off my chair, I was so surprised. Who could be calling me? I slid open my little red phone and answered, "Hello, this is Carmen."

"Hi, Carmen? This is Sarah (not her real name) with Patack. (not the company's real name) . . ."

"Oh, Hi . . . Sarah with Patack." The name sounds familiar, I was thinking.

"Yes, you recently signed up with our company, we are looking for an agent to do BPO's in your area. How many can you do in a day?

My eyes popped out of my head. I've never done one. I have no idea how many I can possibly do in a day. What is the norm? Thoughts were rushing through my head. "How many can you give me?" I asked.

"Well, since you are just starting with us, I can only give you six a day."

My head is computing . . . six times fifty, $300 . . . yay!

"I'll take six." I said. "Once we build a rapport, I am sure I will gain more of your business."

She said, "Looking *forward to it.*"

And this, my friends, is how I really started in the real estate business. I did over 300 BPO's that year. It was very little money compared to the amount of work I was putting in and I never got a listing in all that time. But the best part about it was that I learned so much about each community and their property values and that gave me an edge over any other real estate agent sitting around praying for the market to change. I basically was instrumental in determining market values in my community. This seemed like a big responsibility and it gave me the chutzpah I needed to call myself a real estate agent.

CHAPTER 12

THE BUSINESS OF LEAD GENERATION

Statistically speaking in almost every industry you will close four transactions out of one-hundred leads. So, as a real estate agent if you want to make $60,000 in your first year, if average sale price in your area is $300,000 and a commission split of 50/50, you will have to physically work with 1,960 leads per year. 163 leads per month, 39.20 per week and 7.84 leads per day. Those are the numbers.

Sooner than later, when you do the math, you realize that you are actually not in the real estate business, you are in the lead generation business.

So, where are these leads going to come from? I am sure you have already learned from your post-licensing class, your leads come from your sphere of influence, people you run into on a daily basis, expired lists, for sale by owners, just listed, just solds, and a large portion of them from your internet marketing and social media marketing.

Your sphere is not that large, and you have to call everyone to remind them that you just joined a new industry and while they love you, many of them would think that since you are new, you might not be the right candidate to sell their home, unless you have a way to prove them wrong. And let's admit, your friends and family are not always your biggest supporters. Even though they love you, they are realistic. Here is this ugly word again. *Realism is a disguise for pessimism.*

Expireds, FSBO's, just listed, just sold and internet leads will cost you money. And a lot of aggravation caused by rejection. There is a lot of rejection in dealing with expireds and FSBO's because you are not the only real estate agent who figured out there is potential in calling these leads. In fact, there are a lot of coaches out there who teach this approach and you will find that when calling these leads you are not the first one or the last one even if you start at 7:00 am. So, if you don't have thick skin and are able to handle rejection well, this lead generation technique is not for you. As you can imagine, with my fear of getting on the phone, it was not my preferred modus operandum either.

The National Association of Realtors states that over 94% of buyers start their search online. So, if buyers hang out online, how do we get to them? One of the main ways to generate leads online has been pay per click. Which means you as a marketer will have to master the art of bidding on optimized keywords that will bring your website in front of a large enough audience. With this method, you will only pay if a lead clicks on your website. On average, a brokerage pays $10–$14 per lead depending on the area and the competition. So, if you want to reach your target, your cost out of pocket will be a minimum of $19,600. I am giving you this information because as a new real estate agent it makes no financial sense to invest in leads before you have the systems and the techniques in place to convert these leads.

Direct mail is another source of leads and followed correctly, it can be very profitable because this can be a source for sellers as well as buyers. There is a system to follow and the basis of it is consistency, value and a call to action.

This has been one of my most favorite lead generation strategies in my entire career. I've been doing it since the beginning of my career and I have never stopped using it.

It has a very high rate of predictability provided it is followed strategically.

And then, there is Social Media. This is a dream come true for every single sales marketer, small business owner, real estate agent, mortgage lender and any other sales professional with a relatively small advertising budget.

The cost for social media leads is the lowest in any industry and it is still extremely untapped and unexplored.

Statistically speaking, 90% of the social media users are lurkers. They hang out and watch what others are doing without getting involved. 9% participate by liking, sharing, making comments and only 1% of social media users are actually full participants which means they create and post content. The competition is extremely low and there could be no better time to get involved in social media platforms and maximize on this opportunity. The best part about it is you can get involved in social media absolutely free. Once you become proficient, build a following and become consistent, you can start marketing on social media with paid adds starting at $30–$50 for an add. You can show up as a business on the same level as large corporations with massive budgets.

Yes, of course, there is door knocking and sign calls and open houses, but the amount of leads generated through these avenues does not really justify using an entire paragraph on it. I will mention them anyway because I am a believer in not letting any opportunity go to waste. But I do believe that your time as a real estate agent can be spent in better ways than sitting in an open house or door knocking.

CHAPTER 13

THE MONEY IS IN THE LIST AND THE CRM

What is a CRM and why do you need it? Well, I'm glad you asked. A CRM is a customer relationship management system. It is usually combined with an IDX.

IDX stands for Internet Data Exchange. Every real estate website should have one. An IDX is used to integrate the data from your local multiple listing services straight into your website. So, when your clients search for property on your website, they have a similar accessibility as if they were searching on the MLS, like an agent. A buyer should be able to select a multitude of fields that match the MLS fields and a seller should be updated on his or her area market with active, pending and sold listings. A good IDX will integrate as many fields as possible, although I found that when you come across a good CRM source because they spend all their research and resources in the money-making part, which is the customer relations manager part of the system, they often drop the ball on the IDX. A state-of-the-art CRM will always have a good IDX but a good IDX will not always have a robust CRM. This is not a deal breaker but remember it and be prepared when you go shopping for your next CRM.

And now, let's talk CRM. Why do you even need one? Well, let's put it this way. When all you have is one or two clients, you know what they want, you look for property for them every day, you send them a list of new listings directly from the MLS or they find themselves on Zillow and Trulia looking for properties and they send you the listing they want to see, it's easy. When you are in business long enough and have a list of 100, 500, 1000 or more customers, you will not be able to keep track of their names let alone remember what everyone wants and actually send the listing manually. And unless you keep your clients updated daily, they will go somewhere else. So, this is where your CRM will come in very handy. Remember, you are not the only agent with a good IDX and your leads are not signing up only on your website. The better you are at keeping your leads engaged, the better chances you have to turn them into customers.

Here's one of my rules as a real estate broker; I know I mentioned it before, but it is worth repeating it. *You never let go of any single lead coming your way.* I don't care if they are renters, looking for a trailer or in the market for a million-dollar home. You enter them all in your CRM system. You tag them, you assign them a category according to their urgency and you enter all the info you have on them and you set them up to receive daily email updates with new listings in their criteria.

So, unless they are specifically asking you to decrease the frequency, your clients should receive automated email updates on a daily basis. So, when you are out and about showing properties or meeting with sellers, they will receive emails from you with new specific properties.

If they don't get them from you, they will get them from another real estate agent.

Internet buyers and sellers are a different breed of customers. They move fast and if you are not the one to get back to them as soon as possible they will reach out to someone else. Internet leads want immediate gratification and they have thousands of options if you are not on call. Now, here's the trick. If you reach out to them and they don't get back to your right away, it doesn't mean that they are not interested. I am going to say this again: just because they are not responding to you it doesn't mean that they are not interested. *No answer does not mean No*. There is so much distraction nowadays that it takes six to eight touches for a consumer to acknowledge a sales approach.

You must remember one thing: they are on your website for a reason. And forget about the idea that you don't want to bother them. They found value on your marketing, they signed up, they gave you their contact info, their phone number and email address . . . call them. Text them. Email them. All of them . . . and give them value. Value, Value, Value.

If you handle the CRM part of your business in an effective way, you will be able to increase your conversion rate from the National standard of 4% to at least 6–8%. The success of your conversion rate increase is in part based on how robust your CRM is. The CRM you choose will have to work for you instead of the other way around.

Here's what your CRM should be able to do for you. At any given time, you should be able to analyze your client's status when it comes to estimating how many properties they have looked at, how many times, do they have any favorites, are they reading your emails, are they calculating mortgages or are they sending listings to someone else.

In addition, a good CRM must be able to send automatic emails and texts via drip campaigns. Now, here's the kicker. You want to make sure that these are smart drips not just a series of emails and texts that you turn on and when it ends, it ends. You need to put it all on auto-pilot. A smart drip starts when you change a lead's category as well as when a lead responds. Brilliant, right? So, when you are out showing properties with a lead who's been communicating with you through the system, and you forgot to turn off their drip email, they are not getting a text from you saying "Hey I haven't seen you on the site" while you are both standing in the driveway. So, if you want to increase your conversion rate, this is one of the tools you must implement in your real estate business.

A good CRM should allow you to set up a to-do, integrate with other vendors like Mojo dialers or video forwarding sites like BombBomb, as well as a CMA creating site like RPR. A good CRM should give you a daily list with any leads who contacted you or responded to your emails and texts as well as leads that show interest in properties and spend time on the site.

Your CRM should give insights on any properties that match your leads. This tool is extremely valuable when you are ready to take a listing because you can actually show the seller that you already have buyers in your system that are looking for a property just like theirs.

You should be able to tag your leads, advance search your leads, bulk email and bulk text.

CHAPTER 14

YOUR WEBSITE IS AN EXPENSIVE BUSINESS CARD

Now let's talk about your website. If you only have one website and you followed my previous instructions, the same company who is providing you with a CRM and an IDX, will also be building your website.

What your website really does is act as an expensive business card. It has to match your brand, it has to have a great way to capture leads, an easy way for clients to get in touch with you as well as learn more about you from a personal and business standpoint. Your client will want to know who you are, where did you grow up, what school you went to, if you are married, do you have kids, dogs, how many, what profession were you in before you became a real estate agent? What do you like to do? Surf, dance, paint, golf? What did you eat you for breakfast? Why do you love real estate and what do you love the most about your town?

By the way, I know that splitting your commission

with your broker may seem like outrageous but you have to remember that in addition to the many expenses you will have to pay out of pocket, if you are new and you have no experience, unless you work with a broker who has a vested interest in you making money, you will be hard pressed to find a fellow real estate agents to guide you and mentor you through the process because everything you learn can make you become a better agent and take business away from them.

Yes, you can go to seminars and download programs off the internet and learn a little bit about everything but the downside of that is they all cost money and you may be on a goose chase not knowing which program to sign up for in order to generate business right off the bat and in turn become successful. Been there, done that ... and I didn't even get the t-shirt.

And a few more thoughts about your website is that it has to be easy to navigate, and most importantly has to contain pages and pages of available properties and communities with built-in lead capture systems.

While you market your business on postcards, flyers, signs and most importantly social media, you should be able to share a link from your website with a built-in sign-up form.

It is wise to start shopping for domain names and it is important to consider not only names connected to your area of business but also your farm as well as domain names that are catchy and reflect a marketing strategy like clicknaplesvalue.com, listwithcarmen. com, domain names with the address of a new listing, or reflecting some valuable information related to buying or selling a home. These domain names should be easy to read and write and can be easily forwarded to a link on your main website or to your YouTube channel or your part of social media that contains the information you are referring to.

CHAPTER 15
YOU ARE YOUR BRAND

What is your brand? When you think of your brand you naturally think of website, logo, colors, business card and probably a catchphrase or tag line. And you would be partially correct.

I often hear real estate agents talk about branding themselves. And then they start panicking about the price of a website and logo and professional photos and they get in a rut because they believe they cannot do any business until they have all of the above.

Yes, they are important, and they are necessary but once you have them, your branding is just starting.

The way I look at it, when you think of your brand you first have to decide what do you want your clients to think and feel when they see you? What words do you expect to come out of their mouth when they stumble upon your marketing?

I want them to think of me as someone who is

knowledgeable, reliable, someone who cares, embraces new technology, someone who is confident but also who is not afraid to be vulnerable and open and sincere and is willing to help with anything even if it is not real estate related. Someone who provides value on a daily basis. This is the image I work on promoting or better yet, presenting every single day with every single action I take.

I thrive to express my brand with clarity and conviction, and I expect that what I promote is in line with what my clients think of me when they see me. This is how I see my brand.

When my actions match my message, I have accomplished my goal of branding myself.

Your brand will take form on your website as you add your logo, your tagline, your colors and your professional photo. And while I'm giving you this information, let me add, please, always use a professional photo on your business card, your website and your social media profiles. They cost around $100. If you splurge for a $500 investment you will be able to get a small portfolio and use these photos from your website to business cards to yard signs and park benches but most importantly on social media where people look at your picture before they accept your friendship of, they choose to follow you. Your photo is the first impression and the first impression still count. Start building your brand by using updated photos of yourself.

Another reason why you want to build your brand to stand the test of time is your exit strategy. Yes, there will be a time when you will be ready to check out and wouldn't it be great if you will actually be able to profit from your business even after you retire?

What you have to remember is that you are actually building a business. Like any business, when built solid you can benefit from your business while you are running it, but you can also benefit from your business if you sell it when you decide to retire or choose to do something else in life.

You are probably going to tell me, "Wait a minute, I am not a broker, how can I sell my business?" You don't have to be a broker to sell your business. You are building a database and a solid system. When you are ready to retire you can sell your book of business together with all the systems, contacts, webinars, the rights to photos and videos and future lead generation.

You can sell it outright or you can sign a contract where you can receive a small percentage of all the sales generated from the business either for a determined period of time or in perpetuity.

Or you can partner with the best agent in your team, let him or her run the business and split the proceeds 51/49. 51% for you while you work only as a consultant.

So now you realize how important your brand

is not just for you today in your business but for the future when you are ready to check out and enjoy the coconut money.

PART 4

**THE DISTANCE BETWEEN COMFORT ZONE
AND SUCCESS IS CALLED MASSIVE ACTION**

CHAPTER 16
SOCIAL MEDIA MEANS SOCIAL

Okay, this is where it starts getting juicy. I know what you are saying. What does social media have to do with my real estate career?

Before I start talking about real estate and social media, I want to remind you all that one statement I made in a previous chapter: Business and Pleasure Do Mix. It's called *Bleasure*. Yes, you heard me. The world of privacy, as you knew it, is gone. It is time to show up as our own selves and show our true colors.

If you want to be successful in sales in any industry and specifically real estate, you must have a social media profile and you have to make it public. There are no other simple ways to explain this statement.

So, if you are not willing to accept this fact, a real estate sales job in a fast-moving world of technology, is not for you.

But hang in there. I will explain everything, and I promise it will make sense.

We talked about lead generation earlier in the book and we determined that in order to be successful in sales we need to be proficient in the lead generation business.

Here are the three most important questions you want to ask yourself every day:

1. Who are my clients?
2. Where they hang out?
3. How do I reach them?

Let's answer the first question. **Who are your clients?** In other words, who is your target audience? Men, and women, typically in the United States, probably around your town with an interest in buying or selling real estate.

This subject can and should be further developed but for now, we are just going to address the interest in real estate.

Go deeper into the subject and you will be able to narrow down your niche. With the risk of repeating myself, remember, there's riches in niches.

WHERE DO THEY HANG OUT?

And this, my friends, is the million-dollar question. They hang out on Social Media. Every single day. So, if your clients are on social media, this is where you want to be, grabbing their attention.

I know that numbers can be boring so bear with me while I share with you some statistics to back my story and hopefully to convince you that there is substance in my statements. I will use round numbers for easy understanding.

There are 7.6 Billion People on Planet Earth

4 Billion Internet users

3 Billion Active Social Media users

The Pew Research Center is a nonprofit, nonpartisan fact tank that informs the public about issues, trends and attitudes shaping the world.

In 2005 Pew Research reported that 5% of Americans use Social Media. By 2011 this number rose to 50% and today, in 2018, 69% of all American adults use at least one Social Media platform. These numbers are staggering and there is no going back.

Social media has become a one-stop shop for keeping in touch with friends and relatives, for information, news, entertainment, networking, sharing photos and opinions, inspiration, business, referrals and researching new products.

Here is another statistic to help you with narrowing

down your audience. 88% of adults ages 18–29 use at least one social media platform. 78% ages 30–49, 64% ages 50–64 and 37% ages 65+.

So, if your target client is between the ages of 30–64, chances are 70% of them will be hanging out on at least one platform and this is where you want to be.

Here are the most popular platforms as of January 2018 Pew Research study: 73% Americans are on YouTube, 68% on Facebook, 35% on Instagram, 29% on Pinterest, 25% on LinkedIn and 22% on WhatsApp

How often are these adult Americans visiting their preferred platforms? 74% of all Facebook users visit their platform of choice daily. Let that sink in. 66% daily Instagram users, 45% daily YouTube users and 46% on Twitter daily.

45%, nearly half of American adults get their news on Facebook and 18% on YouTube.

39% of all active social media visitors use a mobile device.

Social media has become a daily routine with 74% of all active users being on Facebook daily and six out of ten being on Instagram daily.

Check out this article for more detailed and updated stats.

http://www.pewinternet.org/fact-sheet/social-media/

In a nutshell, there are 327 million adults in the United States. 68% (222 million) of them use Facebook. 74%, 164 million adult Americans visit their Facebook page at least one per day, every day. Need I say more?

And we can reach these people for free! When it comes to social media interaction there is absolutely no difference between a large multimillion-dollar company and a ma' and pa' business owner. We are using the same playing field and if we don't take advantage of this massive opportunity, we will be eaten up alive. There is absolutely no other platform that comes even remotely close to this statistic.

So, here comes question number three.

HOW DO WE GET TO THESE PEOPLE?

By trading daily valuable content in exchange for your audience attention.

What is valuable content? Your story, education, information, news, entertainment, inspiration and motivation.

You become a media entity. You become a digital agent. Your purposefully crafted content is your way to your client's attention. You trade your content for likes, shares, comments and personal engagement and referrals.

Why you? Because you will become the one and only real estate agent in your client's feed on a daily basis and even if they are not ready to move now, you will be the one they will reach out to when they are or when they know someone else looking to buy or sell.

So, this is where we bring back your brand. Since we determined that your clients are hanging out on social media, our next step is to bleed our brand into the social media platforms of our choice.

When it comes to branding on social media the elements to focus on are your text, your images, your videos and your presence.

Social media represents a type of media in which people interact with each other. Self-explanatory, right? Social means Social. So, just like real-world interactions, social media follows the exact same rules of engagement.

For example: if you walk into your office wearing a beautiful dress and a colleague pays you a compliment, you say, "Thank you, I appreciate it," instead of sticking your thumbs up. If you stick your thumbs up in real life, they'll think you are a jerk and it's the same thing on social media.

Here is another one for you. Say you go to someone's house and ring the doorbell wearing a mask on. Do you expect them to open? I don't think so. So, why would anyone accept your friend request on Facebook when you either don't have a profile photo or the photo is of your dog or your child.

I know what you are thinking now? Which platform should I use? Great question. I have been a Twitter user since 2008, a Facebook user since 2007, I am a baby on Instagram, as I have only been on it since 2017. I started my YouTube account in 2009 and started with Pinterest in 2013. LinkedIn is a very strong business relations platform that has been improving it's interacting tools and should not be neglected in your marketing.

My go-to platforms are Facebook and YouTube. This is where I find my clients, so this is where I spend most of my time and resources. I use Twitter and Instagram periodically and only because I want to have some fun and explore and because I don't want to miss out on anything new.

So, remember, your primary platform of choice should be where your target audience hangs out not where you want to hang out.

So, if I have to give you the best advice on where to start with your social media marketing strategy, you want to start with a public Facebook profile, a business Facebook profile and a YouTube account. Yes, I said public Facebook account. And yes, this means anyone, and everyone can find you and see your posts. And when I say everyone, I mean including your friends, customers and clients.

CHAPTER 17
FACEBOOK IS YOUR BFF

Let's get social with Facebook.

Facebook was founded in February 2004 by a bunch of Harvard students led by a poorly dressed brainiac, Mark Zuckerberg, one of the youngest self-made billionaires in the world. If you see photos of him, you will notice that he wears the exact same thing all the time: a grey t-shirt and a pair of jeans. At times, he will add a hooded sweatshirt to this fashionable ensemble. And while you may think that he never changes clothes, which is something Steve Jobs did for a while in his lifetime, the Facebook boy does it on purpose. He actually owns a closet full of very expensive t-shirts and jeans that look identical. While many of us fashionistas out there may think this is ludicrous, his reasoning makes sense. He says that the least amount of decisions unrelated to the business he has to make on a daily basis, the more chances he has to concentrate on what's important.

Well, more power to him but you will never see me wearing the same pair of shoes two days in a row. Personally, I feel that spending a few minutes every day deciding on style stimulates my creative energy and I believe it actually enhances my brand.

So, whether you like the Facebook boy or not, his creation is here to stay and is growing in popularity every day in spite of hiccups from time to time.

Facebook has been a friendly platform for all of us not only for getting news and memes and watching inspirational or puppy videos. Facebook has been the glue that brought us back together with old high school friends, old relatives, old flings and is helping us every day grow and evolve as human beings.

In 2017, Facebook has helped me bring together my high school friends from Romania and I was able to organize our thirty-year high school reunion from hundreds of miles away. We were 220 people when we met seven months later, and it was the largest gathering of my generation. We did not just have a lot of fun, but we went down the memory lane and learned more about ourselves and our outrageously successful colleagues. We learned that some of my friends were Google and LinkedIn engineers, brain surgeons, professors, psychiatrists, members of Nobel Peace Prize–winning chemistry teams, media producers, law enforcement officials, developers, real estate brokers, politicians as well as mothers and fathers. We were able to meet and appreciate where we came from and how important our teachers were and the sacrifices, we went through to become who we are today. We laughed, we cried, we danced, we reminisce, and we made a promise to see each other again. Without Facebook, this would have never happened. And for this, I think Facebook rocks.

So, let's dive into this platform.

As I mentioned before 90% of Facebook members are lurkers. 9% interact by liking, commenting and sharing and only 1% are actually providing valuable unique content. If you want to stay relevant and make an impact, you want to be in the 1% category.

Here are some of the most common-sense rules of engagement on Facebook.

1. Be nice. Remember, someone is always watching.

2. Do not post ambiguous, alarming and attention getting posts like: OMG, *we are in the ER room and it is so crowded . . .* very annoying to have all your friends show concern and you are nowhere to be found and you show up hours later saying: oh, we went there with my neighbor, all is good now . . . remember the crying wolf story. Or something like: *that's it, I'm done*

with dating ... and no other explanation for days. People don't like this, they think of it as drama and they will stop following you.

3. Private matters should be addressed in messenger and not on your page.

4. Keep the gushing about your marriage and any other personal achievements on the down-low. Nobody wants to be friends with a braggart.

5. Be mindful of what you post and avoid like the plague any religious, political or any other controversial posts.

6. Reply to all comments, not just with a like or love. If someone commented on your posts, you respond back even if it just a quick thank you and an emoji.

7. Comment on your friends' posts. Compliment them when they change their profile photo, or they post photos of their kids and pets. Be polite and courteous. Give your friends some love and you will get it in return.

8. Don't stalk your new friend's profile. Don't comment on every one of their posts. First, it's weird and second, don't you have anything better to do?

9. Do not, ever start a group on messenger without everyone's approval. And if you do, don't be surprised if people will start dropping off like flies. Nobody likes to get notification for every emoji sent out in the group.

10. Do not tag your friends on photos without their permission. This is very important. We all have a better side and if you tag me on a photo of my bad side, you are in trouble. I am joking, of course, but you get the message.

11. Do not vent unless there is something really funny about it or it is self-deprecating.

12. Do not cut and paste status updates that ask you to cut and paste and share with everyone else "if you are my real friend." They are annoying, disingenuous and potentially spreading viruses.

13. Definitely, do not spread chain updates on messenger with the message saying that if you don't share it with ten people, a whole lotta trouble will descend upon you.

14. Do not post any sex or violence related posts.

15. Pay attention not to appear a lush. Photoshop your beer bottle if it appears in all your photos.

16. Do not post about business and tag people who are unrelated to the post. Generally speaking, be very cautious when tagging people, especially when they are not your close friends.

17. Do not tag a whole bunch of people on your posts unless they asked you to do it. They will not only eventually untag themselves, but they may even unfriend you.

18. Don't post on people's walls unless agreed upon. If you want to get their attention on a post, share it to your wall and make a comment with their name in it.

19. Don't complain about other businesses or about any of your clients or friends.

20. Don't steal another friend's content. If you find value in it, just click share and give them credit for it. Mention their name in the comment and you may start interacting with their friends too. Just saying . . .

21. Don't just share. Create your own, authentic content.

22. Don't invite all your friends to like your business page. Chances are they are in the same business as you and they will never be a client. Be selective. Plus, when you post on your main page and share on your

business page, they will end up seeing your post twice.

23. Be mindful of spam. If it looks weird, it probably is. It usually comes in the form of an alarming post or a promise of huge gains if you share to several of your friends.

24. Be mindful of friend requests from people you have no common friends with. Look through their profile and if they just changed their profile photo or header, chances are they are a spammer.

25. Choose your friends wisely. Just by scrolling through the first seven to ten posts on anyone's wall you can usually figure out what they are about. Keep out the negative people, the ones obsessed with politics and controversial subjects. They will only be a distraction for you if you end up seeing their posts daily.

26. Do NOT play games on Facebook and invite others to join you. Playing games on Facebook raises a signal to your clients that you have nothing better to do.

27. Do not post useless information like: *in luggage claim*.

28. Do not post a photo of your food in a restaurant without checking in on that

restaurant and giving some valuable information about the place, the menu or the service . . . preferably positive . . . better yes, if you don't have something good to say about a place, don't say anything . . . remember what your grandmother used to say.

29. Give nine times, ask once. This is the formula for your posts on Facebook. Basically, your main mission will be to provide your followers with value nine times before you ask for anything in return. Giving can be a post, a comment, a share. Likes don't count, sorry. This doesn't mean you should stop liking.

30. Friend people and accept at least ten new friends daily. You can have 5000 friends on Facebook. Max it out as soon as you can. But remember the rule: quality before quantity. Facebook friend suggestions work.

31. Do not wave at new friends but if they wave at you, please answer back with a wave. If they reach out in a way that may seem a little forward or inappropriate, just ignore. They might not be a bad person, just badly mannered. If they annoy you . . . unfollow

and unfriend. Do not get involved in a negative conversation and mostly, do not vet about it on your page.

32. Do not post text only. Always use a photo, a graphic or a video. Here's a great app for you: Bitmoji. I have it downloaded to my phone. I created my own avatar resembling a pretty and young version of myself and I post it for holidays or anytime I don't have something else handy. You will love this app and your friends will be impressed.

33. Emojis ... I can't stress enough how important it is to use them. Make sure they are relevant to the topic of your post. The chance people will read your words will increase if you use relevant emojis.

34. Hashtags. I am sure you all know what they are but if you don't, this is a word or a phrase preceded by a hash mark, like this #, for the sole purpose of having the post identified and indexed by the social media platforms. The good news about hashtags is that your posts are not limited only to your friends but to any social media user. How do you know what hashtags to use? Google best hashtags for real estate. Personally, I don't use a lot of hashtags

because they don't really matter so much on Facebook but if you are an Instagram user, it is a good idea to have at least ten for each post. But when I do, I keep them short and to the point. And if you decide to use them, place them at the end of your post or even as a comment to your own post. Quick tip: separate them by a dot or an asterisk. Rule of thumb, no more than thirty hashtags per post.

CHAPTER 18

VIDEO MARKETING

So, now that we have established the very basic rules of engagement for Facebook, here is the moment you all have been waiting for. How do you actually stand out from the crowd?

By becoming a movie star. Well, not really . . . by learning to create videos and post them on your social media.

Generally speaking, a typical agent will spend in excess of 75% prospecting and converting leads and a lot less time doing customer service and client care. Statistically, spending more time with client care will increase conversion rate and repeat business. So, a better strategy would be to spend 75% of the time on servicing and client care and only 25% of the time on prospecting and conversion.

Going where your clients are which is on social media and providing them with valuable information via video, photos, memes and text is a perfect example of customer care and will increase your conversion rate.

According to an article on HubSpot, video content marketing is expected to claim over 80% of all web traffic by 2019. Wow.

When you add a video in the body of your email, the chances for that email to be opened increases in excess of 250%

https://blog.hubspot.com/marketing/video-marketing-statistics#
sm.0000f7ujhkwrse8sqa62aq63w23fi

Videos are not an up-and-coming marketing strategy anymore. They are here to stay. Not only that consumers love them, but they have become the source of information when it comes to product reviews and feedback, tutorials, webinars, and informational content.

The use of video has extended from YouTube to Facebook to Instagram to Twitter and other social media platforms but most importantly it has placed itself in a prominent spot on email campaign marketing, landing pages, virtual tours, community updates, live open houses and a lot more.

Why should you get on board with video marketing? Because over a third of the time consumers spend online is spent watching videos ... People love watching videos ... and you know what the crazy part is? I am not talking about professional videos ... I am talking about homemade personalized videos that combine information with glimpses of who you really are as a real person.

By using video, you can personally address your client's needs, you can show that you care, that you understand them and that you have the solution for their problem. You can provide value to your client by creating video content related to their needs.

And you show them how you can solve their problem. Once you start showing people that you are capable to solve their problem, to make their dreams come true, your conversion rate will increase, and you will start seeing your dreams come true.

Why video? If you go door knocking, you can probably reach forty homes in two hours. Postcards cost you a lot of money and many of them end up in the trash. Phone calls are becoming obsolete. A video stays online forever and if used and optimized properly you can reach a large audience for a long period of time.

So, here are six reasons why you should start implementing videos in your marketing asap.

1. Leads are more likely to visit your page if you provide them with valuable video content.

2. They are also more likely to share your video particularly if you create the habit of asking them to share it during your vid.

3. Google loves video content so if you have a video on your home page of your website, your SEO will increase, and your website will be found easier.

4. A video can be previewed on any device whether smart phone, tablet or iPad and desktop or laptop.

5. You have a high chance to promote your brand by keeping in line with your core beliefs and values as well as tapping into your niche market.

6. The same two-minute video can become valuable content on a multitude of plat-forms including websites, social media, email campaigns and texting.

In his book, *Jab, Jab, Jab, Right Hook* my favorite marketing guru, Gary Vaynerchuk, said that the only way to stand out in a crowded internet is to provide value in everything you do. Value means free content. Free education and information. Tell them everything and anything you know. Don't worry about the other agents watching and learning from you. Remember, only 1% will actually go ahead and do it. White the book title has only three jabs, Gary's theory is this, give your clients value as many times as possible (this is the Jab) and only ask for a sale once (this is the right hook). I say give nine times and ask once.

I can just hear you say, "What do I say in the video?"

This is where you grab a pen and paper and start taking notes.

Here is a list of ideas for you to use in your video marketing.

Virtual tours showing a series of photos of the home are a thing of the past now. Buyers are simply not watching them anymore as they are boring. Sellers feel that a virtual tour doesn't enhance their home enough and they feel that you as a listing agent are not doing enough for the home. So, if you decide to post a virtual tour, make it a real video narrated throughout with the best highlights of the home.

PROPERTY VIDEOS.

So, the alternative is to combine photos or short videos of the home with videos of yourself describing the best things about the home and why someone should buy it. And this is where you as an agent have the chance to shine. Because the idea is not to start explaining how many bedrooms and bathrooms you are going to show them but why is this home special. Be it the location within the community, upgrades, view, proximity to schools, which schools, what did the seller loved about the home and what will the new buyer enjoy about the home as well, and how they will enjoy their evenings on the patio with friends grilling and sharing old stories. This is your opportunity to make the buyers feel good about the home and the seller will love you.

If you have a cooperative seller, get them interviewed on camera and let them tell the buyers what is it that they love about the home, whether it's the western exposure and it's sunsets, the open kitchen and space around the bar or the way they bring their groceries inside the home through the laundry room and they get to park their bags on top of the washer and dryer. Let them share it all down to the littlest detail. You can edit it later.

And here is another secret. All the neighbors will want you to be their listing agent because nobody else has done this for their home, nobody else has understood them better.

One thing to keep in mind when you post virtual tours on your local MLS listing, you might want to check if they require non branded tours and you can take off your contact information but you can still post the branded version on the popular sites like Zillow, Trulia, Reator.com and your own site as well as YouTube and specifically all social media.

When posting this video, be sure to include your website link of the community and not just of this listing. Why? Because your listing will eventually sell but the video will remain posted and future potential buyers will have a chance to find other properties just like it.

By the way, as soon as your listing sold, be sure to remarket this video as sold and offer a link to similar homes in the area. You missed this home but here's your chance to move into a similar home.

COMMUNITY VIDEOS.

This is your chance to shine. These videos are a very good tool to showcase your expertise. Whether you create a video about your town or about specific popular subdivisions in your area or just the ones in your farm area, you can use this content to not only share it via email and social media, but you can post it on your YouTube channel and optimize it for lead generation.

All you have to do is get as much information as you can gather about each community and put it all together in a video. *Don't just tell them ... show them.*

Get the keys to the clubhouse, community pool and

exercise room and take shots of you running on the elliptical or soaking your feet in the hot tub ... make it fun and entertaining. Give them the content with a glimpse of who you are. Talk about fees, number of units, views, rules, are pets allowed or not, what size pets and can they have a motorcycle. If they can, tell them that. If they can't, tell them that too. And always, always, offer a link from your website in the body of the post with properties available for sale in that community. This is your chance to capture leads.

DRIVE BY COMMUNITY VIDEO.

Another great example of community video is a video that you take while slowly driving through the community, or someone else drives you and you capture the feel of the community and common areas and emphasize the beautiful landscaping or whatever makes that community special. The best part about it is that Google does not go inside gated community when they feature their street views so you can be a pioneer at it in your area. If you want to go above and beyond, you can hire a photographer to take some aerial videos and you can combine them with your other content. This should not cost you more than $150–200 when you hire a photographer.

Then, when a consumer goes online and tries to get information about a specific community, your

YouTube video will show up at the top of search engines. Remember Google loves video and YouTube is owned by Google. Simple. And, you will reap the benefits for ever or for as long as you will be in the business.

MARKET UPDATE VIDEOS

These are the easy ones. Your local area MLS releases quarterly reports. All you have to do is read them, understand them, relate them on video in your own terms as well as go deeper into some of the communities you specialize in and give your audience some insight on the local market in that community. Also, you might want to ask your audience to send you a message if they are interested in the market report of a specific neighborhood and you can customize it for them.

CLIENT TESTIMONIALS VIDEOS

Video testimonials are very powerful especially if you find a client to say some really nice words about you and how you solved their problem. This should not be impossible. Yes, some clients might be apprehensive to get on camera, but someone will, just ask. A video testimonial from a client is Money with capital M.

And, you can edit the video with shots of your client at the closing table, doing the walkthrough and shots of the property. Be sure if you include shots of the property, they are the ones you took and not from the MLS, as they belong to the other agent.

LOCAL BUSINESSES VIDEOS

This is your opportunity to become the digital mayor of your town. You can showcase all kinds of businesses in your local area, from restaurants to spas, shops, farmer's markets and any local events. These videos can be a valuable source of information for your existing clients as well as for future customers.

When it comes to these types of videos, consistency is key. Not only that your clients find value and come back to your page or your vlog to see what else is going on in town but you will also have businesses reach out to you so you can feature them on your page.

Now, here's how you do this. You reach out to the business, film a chef in the kitchen or a bartender fixing drinks and start a game of trivia. Whoever guesses the price of a cocktail or a meal will receive a free appetizer next time they are in the restaurant.

So, basically having a video of a restaurant or store is not enough, and your job becomes engaging the audience and providing value, which is the free appetizer or a specific discount at the jewelry store or furniture store since your clients will be moving soon. And, you will get to check in at that location so all the business followers and clients will get to see your post and like, comment or share your post. Hint: these are the people you will want to friend.

INTERVIEWS

Interviews are a very powerful video tool as well. So, you can come up with a series of questions and you meet with your preferred inspector, mortgage lender, title company or attorney, an appraiser, a property management company who handles the CAM in a community, a home watch person. Every one of these people can shed some light and clarify some of your client's concerns. Your only job is to bring these issues to light and deliver the content to your audience.

Now, remember, don't just show up for the interview. Come up with some great questions and make them relate to issues that you already had in your transactions or that your clients have expressed concerns about.

Where do you post these videos? On Facebook, on YouTube, on your website, or your vlog. And be sure to tag the people interviewed and their business. They will generate more leads for you.

HOME IMPROVEMENT VIDEOS

And this is where you can video any of your clients who are buying a fixer upper and show what can be done to improve a property and bring it to contemporary standards. Bring in a contractor who specializes in remodels and get him to speak about the upgrades he can bring and pricing. This will really help you sell other dated homes and build a relationship with the contractor. People love before and after so be sure to have some of those. The contractor will be happy to give them to you but be sure to have them sign a release so you can use the video anywhere you want, and if your video gets millions of views on YouTube, they are not going to come after you for the money you make from advertising. Insert LOL here. *Dare to dream.*

LIVE VIDEOS

These are the hot ticket and once you start doing them, you will be addicted. The easiest thing possible. You don't have to do anything. No editing, no posting, no cover page, nothing. Just get online and start saying things that matter but do think value and give it to your audience wrapped up with a smile and bow. You can do live videos at an open house, interview someone you have announced prior to the post, you can do an interview while you meet them in person or you can invite someone to join your live from a remote location. So basically, you can bring in one of your affiliates and ask them questions on live video.

One of the best things about a live video is that every single one of your friends who is online at the time you are posting will get a little red box pop up telling them that you are online . . . and they can't help it but push the button and start watching you.

And by the way, when they do, you do not need to acknowledge them. In fact, if they have never watched a live video before, do now yell out loud, "Hey Joanna, thank you so much for joining me today." They will freeze, they will freak out and not know what to do because they will think that somehow you are watching them. And the next time you're live, they will think twice before they push the button.

If they interact, acknowledge and thank them for being with you but don't turn it into a conversation.

And, it is okay to start a live video and continue it before any number of people show up to watch. Remember, they can always watch later.

And I will give you another valuable piece of advice. Before you push live, go ahead and type in a little description of what the post is going to be about. It will help anyone who stumbles upon it later, as it will give them an idea if they are interested or not in turning the sound on. Be lively and entertaining and you will get a huge following.

AGENT PROFILE VIDEO

This is a video you can actually use as an introduction to all your new leads signing up on your website. You can set it up as a drip email so they can get is a few minutes after they log in. One of the best ways to set it up is to record it in your office or on location, maybe in one of your nice listings or a model home and upload it to BombBomb. This is an amazing app you can integrate with many CRM's and it embeds your video in the body of the email, so your recipient doesn't actually have to click on a link to go to it. If you create the video, start with a short shot of you holding a piece of cardboard in your hand. Write something fun on it like *click here, I don't bite*. I don't know . . . I just made that up. Really just write, click for your message or something like that and move the cardboard left and right with a smile on your face. This will attract their attention and they will want to turn on the video.

HOW TO VIDEOS

This is where you offer practical information about selling or buying a home.

When it comes to selling, you offer tips on how to get a home ready to be sold. How they can improve a curb appeal, how they can paint, clean up, declutter, etc. If you actually send this video to a seller you are going to meet with, they already know what to expect so you're in business. Not a lot of resistance when you start asking for the magnets to come off the fridge. You emphasize in the video that the buyers will want to feel themselves at home and the more personal items they see in the home, the less chance they have to see the home as theirs, plus the more stuff they see, the less chance they have to actually look at the home as opposed to the memorabilia.

When it comes to buying, what are the tips on making offers, how to buy sight unseen, how to buy as is and get a credit for repairs. You can be creative about it and you can start by reminiscing every single one of your transactions you had in the past and draw ideas from it.

If you are new to the business, meet with one of your colleagues and ask them to give you ideas. Chances are they'll laugh in your face, but you never know, sales people love talking about themselves.

INSIGHT VIDEOS.

Okay, these are money. Capital M. These videos are the ones you use to drip your clients and let them know exactly what they can expect when buying or selling. I am talking about getting pre-approved, making the offer, asking for concessions, what to know about inspection, appraisals, mortgages, contingencies, closing costs and the rest of the whole nine yards.

You do this for buyers and for sellers. You can record them all in one day. These are short two to three minutes videos that will just entice them to want to work with you but will give them enough information and value that they will feel that they learn from you and they can trust you.

CHAPTER 19

WHAT LOCAL ENTREPRENEURS ARE SAYING ABOUT VIDEO AND SOCIAL MEDIA

Over the years, I have been watching several local business leaders using video and social media. These are the pioneers of their industry in our local market and they never cease to inspire me with their courage and dedication.

I reached out to them and asked them a few questions trying to find out their opinion about the value they are getting from this type of marketing.

Here are just a few I would like to acknowledge and thank them for leading the way and showing us all not only that it can be done but that their actions are contributing to their success.

My friend **Sue "Pinky" Benson is a real estate agent with RE/MAX** as well as a National Speaker and a two times BombBombVideo Influencer winner and Inman Contributor. She was gracious enough to share with me a few words that will give you all a good reason to want to push the record button. Here's Pinky: "After moving to a new area and having to basically start my entire real estate career over from zero, I found doing videos with social media was a way for me to stand out from the crowd. It pushed me out of my comfort zone by making me go explore my new town and introduce it to my viewers. They learned about beautiful Naples, Florida right along with me. They suggested places for me to check out. They invited me to get to know them and this beautiful community. Don't be afraid to do something no one else is trying or doing. You honestly have nothing to lose and everything to gain. Cliché but true. We either evolve or dissolve. What will you do?"

In 2017, we had a major storm in Naples and Sue went the extra mile for her clients posting live videos letting them know that their homes are okay. I reminded her about that story, and she said, "During a time when our community was desperate for information, I felt the need to share what was going on and I used FB live to do that. My thoughts weren't 'wow this will get me business in the future.' It was truly a way to share with others near and far what was going on. I was happy I was able to do something to help."

Pinky's business has been growing exponentially since her involvement with video and Social Media and she has real numbers to share: "Using video has grown my business and my brand exponentially. It's hard to gauge ROI on social media period. Video or otherwise. What I can say for myself is that in the last year I've doubled my transactions; tripled my income and 95% of my business comes from social media and referrals from people around the world."

You can find Pinky on her social media platforms at https://www.facebook.com/PinkyKnowsNaples/ and @pinkyknowsnaples on Instagram

Here is what **Jon Bates, owner of Addicted to Fitness,** Naples, FL had to say, "I've had my business open for seven years today. I have successfully used social media to market and brand my business. My stats show that at least 70% of my business has come from Facebook marketing. Social media is where people's attention is right now. If you want to be relevant in business, you have to put yourself out there with a consistent and persistent message. People want to do business with someone they feel they know and like. You have to share your passion with others. Social media is a very effective way to network and get your message out to your customers, current and future. You have to be the one who people think of as the expert in your field. Social media is a place to educate, motivate and inspire others to join your mission. It takes a lot of work and dedication to keep your content going on a daily basis. When you own and operate a small business social media is another job in itself. *It works if you work it.* You can't just put out content and then not engage with your followers. It is very time consuming but so worth the time. Jump in on the social media train or get left behind." What an awesome and inspiring statement. You can join Jon on his page at https://www.facebook.com/jon.bates.522fitcoach

Renee Hahn, Real Estate Agent with Caine Premier Properties uses Social Media and Video as a visual business card, so her clients get to know and trust her before they actually meet, "In my real estate business, I use video and social media as a way to allow people to get to know me from a far. In real estate, people are not only looking for expertise, but there is also a trust factor involved. Social media and video help start that process before I get a chance to meet my future customers in person." When asked which of her posts get the most interaction, Renee said, "The posts I get the most interaction on are ones with humor." Renee is not able to quantify the ROI of her Social Media and video interaction, but she made a statement that is in line with all my findings: I don't know that I can attribute quantifiably the effect. Because it's much more branding than sales. Of course. I get a lot of feedback from the public and also from other agents." You can follow

Renne on Facebook @ https://www.facebook.com/renee.hahn2

Cylie Svartoies with Florida Agency Network is full of positive energy and her posts engage hundreds of followers every single time. Here is Cylie's statement, "Video leverages the multiplier effect so people all over the world can be falling in love with you while you sleep, vacation or hustle. I often find people are nervous to hit the record button for fear their message won't come out correctly or that their hair isn't perfect. But here's the thing: you DO have value to add and a message to share, no matter what industry you're in. *Your audience can't love you if you don't hit record. Let them love you!"*

I asked Cylie how she overcame her fear of the video camera.

Here are her inspiring tips for you: "1) I started doing a live video a day for thirty days on Periscope (back when it was bigger), so my friends weren't on there. It took the pressure off and people would ask me questions during the video, so all I had to do was answer their questions and bam! It created longer videos and more content, and my fear would shrink. 2) When I would go live on FB, I remembered that my friends already knew what I looked like in person, and how I talked, so even if I wasn't having a great hair/

makeup day, I was just talking to friends. 3) I would stand and dance or wiggle or jump to get my energy up before hitting record, so the energy came off during the video, as opposed to sitting and not moving. 4) I remind myself that if we were to meet in person, we'd be friends and they'd love me. If I don't hit record, they may never know me, so I have to hit record to "let them love me." Sounds silly but it helps the most."

Please follow Cylie on Facebook at https://www.facebook.com/cylies and Instagram @cylie_with_a_c

Rachel Rango is my friend at Movement Mortgage and she wanted to share her truly inspiring story about her decision to embrace video and social media . . . here is Rachel, "Before I sat down to write this, I was looking over my "Facebook Memories" and just one year ago today, I filmed one of my very first videos during the start of my career with Movement Mortgage. My manager, Jonathan Garrick randomly popped his head into my office and said, "You have a big online presence. I think it's time you do a video and let people know why you made the switch to Movement." That flash of fear and a sudden feeling of sickness took over my body completely and I imagine I turned ghost white. However, this was my new boss and I have got to impress him with my courage!

Looking back on that video now, it's obvious that I

was nervous. I stumbled over my words a little bit and moved my hands around awkwardly as I was trying to convey my story. What's great about it is that it was raw and authentic. The story I told was real and the reasons why I made the switch to Movement Mortgage are the same thoughts I have today.

Since then, my goal was to burst out of my comfort zone and hit the social media game hard. I am incredibly proud of who I am and how I can help people achieve their dreams and social media is just the platform for me to shout it off the rooftops to the world. When I started in this career, I was told that everyone, no matter where you go or who you're talking to, should know what I do for a living. Anyone at any point, for either themselves or someone they know, will need a mortgage at some point. By continuously posting videos, pictures, and going Facebook live, I'm able to stay top of mind to all of my social media audience.

Social media has certainly helped me grow my business. I get messages all the time from friends, realtors, or even strangers requesting information, help, or just general questions. I've closed deals for friends I haven't talked to in years. Recently, I randomly messaged an old friend about their business, and afterwards they asked me about a home loan since seeing my posts. We closed on his house last month. My other favorite part is simply shopping for groceries and someone I don't recognize says, "Hey! You're Rachel Rango. I see your videos all the time. You're truly an inspiration." Social media is certainly an aggressive tool that can take your business to the next level and I'm living proof." Thank you, Rachel.

Michele "Bee" Bellisari is a real estate extraordinaire in Boca Raton. We have been friends on Facebook for a few years and she inspired me to jump in with both feet. Here is what Michele has to say, "Social media and video, in particular, allow us to build a "visual" community to share our lives and business through. At any time and any age, you can build your personal brand, become a resource and surprise and delight people through the use of social media. Pick up that phone and just do it!"

I asked Michele, *"How did it affect your business and how long have you been doing it?"*

Her answer, "I've been doing social media since Facebook started pretty much. The visibility it has given my real estate business and my personal brand is hands down the best way I could have marketed my businesses. I really went full on with Snapchat for the video and started doing Facebook Lives as soon as it showed up. Customers find me and I get referrals from social media for both my businesses."

Her key takeaway, "Midlife mama #over50 is no

excuse to not be doing social media for your business . . . if I can do it so can you!"

Michele "Bee" Bellisari -RE/MAX Services and #SoooBoca Lifestyle & Media
You will find Michele on Social Media at:
https://www.facebook.com/michelebellisari
Instagram @themichelebee
Michele's blog: https://soooboca.com/

Thank you, Michele.

And one last influencer I want to share with you, **Ruth Ahlbrand.** I met Ruth at #Agent2021 in Miami and she blew me away with her knowledge, expertise, and energy.

Here is a little bit of what Ruth has to say, "My life has been all about technology and being on the cutting edge. I love creating and teaching.

In 2009, my husband was diagnosed with stage 4 throat cancer. We decided to increase our property management business for more income so he would not have to work If he was not cured.

We also decided that I would start my dream website company to build a site for Realtors. We produced marketing videos to describe the many facets of the site. I knew content and videos were the key component with a CRM that "automagically" sends emails to captured buyers, sellers, investors, and renters. Why? Agents get too busy. The content and videos fit right into social media. I stuck to design and purpose which is: the website is for the consumer to learn and love Las Vegas.

When you look at LasVegasRelocation.com you will know what I'm saying. I create marketing videos to use in the FB ads for warm leads.

My DNA is threaded with positivity, strength, love, and a longing to live a long healthy life.

I wake up happy and anxious to keep climbing."

Ruth is 72 years old. So, for any of you out there using age as an excuse, please go ahead and visit Ruth's Facebook profile.

Ruth Ahlbrand
RE/MAX CENTRAL
Facebook.com/Ruth.ahlbrand

Ruth, you ROCK.

CHAPTER 20

HOW TO RECORD A VIDEO

Now that we have eliminated all our limiting beliefs, we decided that we can actually do this and become relevant in our industry, let's get technical, shall we?

First of all, you want to make sure you own a smartphone. I personally prefer an iPhone, but a Samsung will work just fine.

Second, I highly recommend some type of tripod or stabilizer.

My favorite tripod is sold by a company I found on Facebook . . . go figure . . . called socialite-lighting.com. You can buy a telescopic tripod and a light for anywhere between $50–$150.

Once you start getting used to the process of recording your own videos, you want to consider a gimbal stabilizer. My go to one is the DJI Osmo Stabilizer or a Smove GoPro and they cost me around $150 on Amazon.

There is nothing more annoying than a live video or a recorded video without a stabilizer. The stabilizer will remove all the vibration from your video, and you can record while in motion, making it possible for your audience to watch without a pack of Dramamine.

Most of these devices come with a small remote that can easily be set up to interact with the phone so you can push the record button from steps away. This will give you a more relaxed look and it shows that you are in control of the recording. If you don't have the option to set the remote up, don't worry, you will always be able to edit your video before publishing it.

No matter what you do, you have to make it simple so it will be sustainable and duplicable. You are not a videographer, you are a real estate agent and you are not changing careers. Keep it simple and go with what you've got.

Using raw footage and simple videos will make your approach more authentic and in turn more relatable. You show up as a real person as opposed to a marketer. Your clients will like this and appreciate your efforts.

The next very important aspect of video recording is setting up the right background. Again, you do not need a professional studio, but you also don't want to start recording inside your bathroom. You want to make sure you have a pleasant background, preferably simple, without distraction but know that a plain blank wall is not a good idea either. A nice office look with a bookshelf behind or a corner showing a window with closed blinds, a plant, a work of art would be ideal.

Of course, the other choice of background will be on location. Which means, in front of a building, inside of a home, on the street, beach, etc. Please remember to choose a location without any background noise. In fact, you must even avoid recording a video on a windy day. You'll easily be able to figure out the problem if you listen to your video after you recorded it, but you will be frustrated and have to record it again. The worst part is when you go live, and the background noise is distractive enough that people will tune out.

No matter where your shooting location is, a very important thing to remember is lighting. If you are indoors, be sure to have a good light in front of you. In fact, the Socialite lighting system comes with two kinds of lighting: one for a tall tripod which I highly recommend and one for just your phone when you shoot remotely. This one runs on battery and can be carried in your purse so you will always have a handy lighting equipment. Ladies, when it comes to good lighting, don't cheap out. You'll thank me later.

One other tool I rarely use is a microphone. This is a great tool if you record in places that tend to have some background noise or to cancel out some of the room's echo. A very good mike to use is a lavalier mic and I found Giant Squid Audio Lab Omnidirectional microphone to have some of the best reviews. Personally, I have never used a mic other than a desk one.

So, just to recap. You'll need a phone with a good resolution camera like a more recent iPhone or Samsung, a tripod, a gimbal stabilizer, lighting equipment and at times, you may use a mike. I hope you already have the phone so your future investment should be the tripod, the light and the stabilizer, in this exact order. Please know that if you are determined to make this work, a $9 tripod from Office Depot will do the trick. Do not use the lack of money to buy all these products as an excuse for you to fail at this crucial step in your business.

Here are a few very important extra tips on recording a video or going live.

When you record a video, you always want to hold your phone in a horizontal position. This way the screen is wider, and you get a lot more coverage. Plus, because you will be posting all these videos on your Facebook page and your YouTube channel, the video will have a more appealing look if it is horizontal.

When you go live, be sure to keep your phone in a vertical position unless you invite a guest during your live and you want to split the screen which is really cool. If you go live on your own and you forget to record vertically, you will come up sideways. Not ideal.

Whether you go live or record a video, please make sure to **always** look inside the tiny little dot where the camera is. This is the only way you will actually speak to your audience as opposed to looking at their chest. This is actually one of my biggest pet peeves when a seasoned video marketer does not make eye contact. It shows me that they either don't know what they are doing, or they don't care about their audience. What do I do in this case? I tune out. You do not want to fall into this category, or you will lose your tribe and you are wasting your time and energy.

You can also go live on your desktop or laptop devices. The process is the same, but your video will actually come up horizontally and it will be a lot more effective for you when posting it on your YouTube channel.

So, please remember, the key is to upload your video on your Facebook page, your YouTube channel as well as a video blog created on WordPress which you can easily access from your mobile device. These sites are inexpensive, and you can actually build them on your own. The main reason why you want to own a video blog ... or a vlog is because you want to own your own content just in case something majorly wrong happens with the social media platforms or YouTube. The other reason you want to have your own platform to post all these videos is because you will eventually have to delete them off your phone and you want to be able to access them at any given time. And, again ... you do not need a vlog in order to get your video marketing. Do not use this excuse to slow you down. As my mother used to say when I grew up, it will all happen in due time. I am just mentioning this to you, so you are prepared.

And just to throw you another curveball, every time you post or upload your videos, you want to give a little synopsis of what the video is about. Make it short, fun, be sure to include emojis and a call to action. Also, make sure to add any of the hashtags that pertain to the subject of the video.

CHAPTER 21

HOW TO CREATE A THUMBNAIL PEOPLE WILL WANT TO CLICK ON

When I first started creating videos of myself, I was awkward, fearful, stiff and long winded. Well, you kind of know why I was fearful but the reason why I was long winded is because I did not know how to cut out the parts that were irrelevant.

In fact, you can still watch one of my cooking videos on YouTube in which I am chopping red peppers really, really fast explaining that the reason I am so fast is because I don't know how to edit the video and I don't want to make it too long. Yes, it would be funny if I was only doing for myself, but I am sure I lost some customers because of it.

Editing a video seemed an act of Congress to me at that time.

That is until my friend Jackson Hardin, whom I met at one of the Tony Robbins events I went to, spent time with me one day and said he was willing to give me a coaching session for free and help me with my videos. Jackson is an amazing personal coach and his offer came in like a gift from God.

Of course, I took him up on it and in just over an hour he gave me a few tips that absolutely changed my life and gave me the confidence I needed to break through and take control of my video marketing.

And this is one of the reasons I am writing this book. Because I feel that it is my obligation to share all this knowledge with everyone who is willing to make a change in their lives.

One of the first tips Jackson shared with me is how to create the cover image of my videos, also known as the thumbnail.

What is the thumbnail and why should you care? The thumbnail is the business card of all your videos. If your video was a book, it's the cover of the book. It is the outfit you wear for a first business encounter. It is the first impression that your video makes and like all first impressions, it matters.

A thumbnail can be an image or a short video accompanied by text. My preferred thumbnail is an image. Mainly because it is simple to produce, and I can duplicate my work and save time.

Your thumbnail is your first chance to hook your audience and make convince them to watch your video. It can be the one and only thing that can turn your audience into customers. In just a few words, it has to be catchy and impressive enough to deliver a call to action, which is: watch me, watch me . . .

Here are a few tips to creating a powerful thumbnail.

1. Use a photo that stands out. Make sure your face is on it and you are looking directly into the camera. You can employ facial expressions that express emotions somehow relevant to the video like surprise, shock, happiness etc.

2. Use a short text message to summarize the content of the video and catchy enough to make your audience curious enough to see what you have to say. Use bold and contracting colors. Studies showed that color yellow is one of the most performing colors and triggers the most clicks to any content.

3. Use graphics if they are relevant to the video. Throw in a beach umbrella or a palm tree if you are presenting a property close to the beach.

4. Be sure to pay attention how each platform uses the space on the thumbnail. For example, YouTube uses the lower right corner for the timestamp and sometimes you will see the play button right in the

middle of the photo. My rule of thumb (pun intended) is: stay away from the lower right corner and keep your face and main message off centered . . .

5. And finally, the importance of consistency. As you start getting good and video and you start building a library, you will want your videos to have a certain look that is specific to you. Something that is easily recognizable. Either similar colors, same text size and font, same logo etc. You will want to eventually incorporate part of your brand on the look of your thumbnail.

Every thumbprint is unique so your video thumbnail should be unique too. Having said that, do not fret over your brand or the consistency of your look when you first start your videos. Do not use this as an excuse to slow you down and delay your success. As you start creating and posting your videos, you will be inspired to come up with a look and you have the luxury to go back and edit your videos on most platforms. Hopefully, you will be too busy recording more and working with clients and you will not have time for such trivial exercise.

I can hear your question, "How to I actually create a thumbnail?" Very easy: you download Canva to your phone. Canva is probably the most impressive free app I have ever encountered.

First, you want to make sure that at the time you recorded your video, you also took a couple of selfies that qualify as a thumbnail. If you have not done it at the time of recording, don't worry, you can always take a screenshot of the best look you can get out of your video and use that photo.

Second, you open Canva, you upload the photo you chose for the thumbprint and you start adding text, shadow boxes and if you prefer, graphics. I am not a big user of graphics, I prefer a cleaner image with a bigger message. You choose your font and colors from the dropdown menus and once you are happy with the results, you download it to your phone.

And that's it, you just created your thumbnail.

You can also log in on Canva.com from your computer and process your thumbnail at a larger scale if you prefer.

A little bit more about Canva. Canva is a graphic design tool for dummies. Over 7 million people use it and I promise you, this tool will become your best friend. It is a cloud-based system so you don't need to download a software and if you open it on your different devises it will sink in so if you start your work on your iPhone or iPad, you can continue it on your computer. You can create memes, banners, flyers, posters, book covers, postcards, business cards, letters, social media headers and posts, you name it . . . there is a template for it. You really don't need to know anything about graphic design. All you have to do it choose, drag, drop, insert and upload your own photos. How do they make money? They have a huge amount of free content as well as a multitude of $1 images and templates if the free ones are not your fitting your style.

CHAPTER 22

HOW TO EDIT YOUR VIDEO LIKE A PRO

The moment you've all been waiting for. Editing your video.

Here is another awesome tip from my friend Jackson Hardin. Another app you can use for free on your phone as well as on your computer. It is called Movie Maker Movavi. I have tried several other video editing platforms and I found Movavi to be the easiest to use, the fastest and the most versatile.

All you have to do is open your app on your phone and follow the instructions. The app is self-explanatory, and it starts by prompting you to choose a photo or a video to upload. You will want to upload your thumbnail if you created it already. If you did not, you can go ahead and edit upload your video and you can create your thumbnail after and upload it at the end.

Once you click on photo or video, the app will prompt you to choose an aspect ratio. This means you can choose to create a video for Instagram, edit one of your live video downloads which is typically vertical or a standard widescreen video, which will be your most common type of video edit.

Once you uploaded your thumbnail followed by your video or series of videos, as you start watching your video, you can stop by simply pushing the stop button or by touching the video. As you determined the part you want to take out, you click on a little scissors symbol and move forward to determine the end of the part you want to crop. You stop again, click on the scissors and gently swipe down the part you don't need to use.

You can stitch together as many videos as you want, and you can add a little bit of text or graphics on any of the parts as well as a musical background for your entire video.

Depending on how long you want your video to be, you can eliminate little parts of the video that are not necessary, or you can crop your long video into short snippets you can use on platforms like Twitter or Instagram. This way, you can record one video and create multiple pieces of content.

Content is king so the more content you create and post on your social media platforms, the better chance you have to reach more customers and get more attention. As Gary Vaynerchuk would say . . .

trade content for attention and you will be successful in any business.

Once you are happy with your video, download it on your photo album. From there you can easily post it to your Facebook, YouTube, your vlog and any other platforms you like.

Generally speaking, the length of your video is determined by the platform you posted on. You can create your video as long as you want them, but you want to keep in mind that we live in a fast-paced world and your audience wants instant gratification. Studies showed that ideal Instagram videos are thirty seconds, Twitter forty-five seconds, sixty seconds on Facebook and two minutes on YouTube. Personally, I have never been able to keep my videos under 3 minutes and I actually post the same video on Facebook as well as YouTube. I crop the content to just the most important part and deliver a shorter video on Twitter and Instagram.

Your live videos can be informational or Q&A's and they will obviously run a little longer. Just remember, if you run your live videos on your computer, you can save the video, download it to your computer and edit it to create content for all the other platforms or for your archive to rerun it when you don't feel like putting any makeup on or you have a bad hair day.

How often should you post? Every single day.

More than once. You have multiple platforms and you don't necessarily have to post on all every day but on your main two, Facebook or Instagram and YouTube, you should post daily.

Times to post? Ideally, you want to post between 9:00 am and 5:00 pm on Facebook and later in the day on Instagram. There is a pretty nifty app called WhenToPost that will give you great insight on when your friends are likely to watch your videos on Instagram. You're welcome.

YouTube's ideal post time is weekdays early afternoon if you have subscribers. And, speaking of subscribers, when you post on YouTube, be sure to always ask people to subscribe to your channel.

CONCLUSION

Harvard Business School Marketing Professor
Theodore Levitt once said, *"People don't want to buy a quarter-inch drill. They want to buy a quarter inch hole."*

This simple quote can be your catalyst to take action in changing the way you sell properties or any other product. When selling a house or helping a seller, you actually sell a dream. A dream of home ownership, a dream of hanging out with friends around a backyard fire, a dream of moving closer to grandchildren or transferring for a better job.

Starting with the end in mind is the substance of everything we decide to do in life including selling properties.

Einstein was right when he said everything is energy including ourselves. The Universe is in perpetual vibration and while it vibrates, it changes. With it, we change too. Once you realize this, you accept and embrace the constant change in yourself you will be able to change your own Universe.

Accepting that the world around us is changing and that we need to change with it is the first step in freeing yourself of the fear of change and the unknown.

Humans survived by being resilient over time and understanding that change happens at a faster pace than ever before can easily help you convert your anxiety into anxiousness. Use the feeling you have while change happens and label it differently. Instead of feeling anxious because of the new world is moving at a fast pace, feel anxious and excited for what is to come and how you can experience more fully the gifts heading your way. Think of all the change coming as a fast morphing of an egg into a caterpillar into a chrysalis and into a beautiful butterfly.

Have the courage to stand up to yourself and decide to believe in yourself. You don't need the approval of your friends, your family, or peers. All you need is your own approval. If your gut feeling tells you to do something, your opinion is the only one that matters.

"*Whether you think you can or whether you think you can't, you're right,*" said Henry Ford.

What I say is this: *If you think you can, you will. If you think you can't, you won't.* Your thoughts dictate your reality.

If you want an amazing reality, have amazing thoughts. It's that simple.

So, go out there, open up like a butterfly, listen and understand your clients and they will choose you and open up to you.

If you are afraid to show up being yourself remember these words *"If I want to be free, I gotta be me."* I did not say it, Bob Proctor did. Or if you prefer a more down to earth philosopher, listen to Popeye, the Sailor Man, *"I am what I am"*.

Yes, you are who you are. You look the exact same way on video as you look in real life. You talk to your friends and customer in real life. Why wouldn't you address them in a video? It's the same thing. You just don't see them. They are inside that little dot called camera. So, all you have to do, just like my friend Cylie, look at the little camera and imagine yourself talking to one of your best friends, preferably someone you know loves you for who you are.

Have faith in yourself. Have faith that you are able to make it through all the changes in the world and be not just a survivor but a winner. Fear doesn't serve and it will not take you anywhere in life. Get rid of fear. The only way you can do that is to strengthen your faith in yourself.

Believe in yourself. I believe in you.

This is not the end . . . this is the beginning.